STUDIES IN RUSSIAN MUSIC

GLINKA

STUDIES IN RUSSIAN MUSIC

CRITICAL ESSAYS ON THE MOST IMPORTANT OF RIMSKY-KORSAKOV'S OPERAS, BORODIN'S "PRINCE IGOR," DARGOMIZHSKY'S "STONE GUEST," ETC.; WITH CHAPTERS ON GLINKA, MUSSORGSKY, BALAKIREV AND TCHAIKOVSKY.

By

GERALD ABRAHAM

COPIOUSLY ILLUSTRATED BY MUSIC EXAMPLES.

Essay Index Reprint Series

BOOKS FOR LIBRARIES PRESS, INC.
FREEPORT, NEW YORK

First Published 1936
Reprinted 1968

To

M. D. Calvocoressi

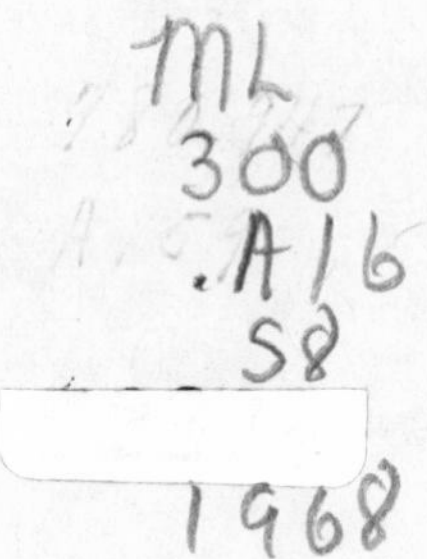

LIBRARY OF CONGRESS CATALOG CARD NUMBER:
68-20285

PRINTED IN THE UNITED STATES OF AMERICA

PREFACE.

ALTHOUGH this is a book of separate essays, it is, I hope, given a certain unity by the fact that each chapter deals with some product or aspect of the "classical" period of Russian music: the music of Glinka and, more particularly, that written in the half-century following his death. I have almost ignored Mussorgsky and Tchaïkovsky, preferring to concentrate on the less discussed members of the "mighty handful," above all on Rimsky-Korsakov who has hitherto been unaccountably neglected by non-Russian critics. But in these studies of some of Korsakov's operas I have concerned myself only with certain aspects of them—perhaps too exclusively—in the attempt to investigate the working of the composer's musical mind.

I have assumed that the reader has some knowledge of the plots of most of the operas discussed. After all, information of that kind has long been obtainable from such books as Rosa Newmarch's "Russian Opera" and Montagu-Nathan's "History of Russian Music." On the other hand, owing to the expensiveness of scores I have used musical examples more lavishly than would be necessary in discussing music which the reader is likely to have in his library.

My Russian spelling is a transliteration rather than a phonetic rendering, though not a *completely* consistent transliteration. It must be remembered that consistency or phonetic accuracy would necessitate "Kyui" or "Kwee" for "Cui." "Chaykovsky" may be the most sensible spelling of that composer's name, but in practice it is almost as irritating to the eye as the horrible "Tschaïkowsky." "Chaliapin" and "Scriabin" are too familiar to be superseded by the more consistent "Shalyapin" and "Skryabin." But on the whole I have followed the system recommended by the Conference of University Teachers of Russian and other Slavonic Languages. The "shch" in "Khovanshchina" looks terrifying but can be managed easily enough by anyone who can pronounce the words "English church" or "fresh cheese."

Five of these essays—the first, second, fifth, sixth and ninth—have already appeared in slightly different forms in "Music and Letters," and a sixth, that on "Prince Igor," in the New York "Musical Quarterly," and my grateful thanks are due to the Editors for their permission to reprint them. The rest are new.

I am also indebted to Messrs. Boosey and Hawkes for permission to quote extensively from works published in the Belaïev and Bessel Editions, for which they are the English agents.

G. A.

CONTENTS.

LIST OF ILLUSTRATIONS.

STUDIES IN RUSSIAN MUSIC.

I.—THE ESSENCE OF RUSSIAN MUSIC.

THERE can be little doubt that the immediate and overwhelming success of Russian music when it first entered the orbit of the English concert-world in the eighteen-nineties was entirely due to its more obvious and superficial elements, its colour and general picturesqueness. As Parry said, it "naturally appealed to the awakening intelligence of the musical masses by vehement emotional spontaneity, orgiastic frenzy, dazzling effects of colour, barbaric rhythm and unrestrained abandonment to physical excitement." But if it had had no qualities other than these to recommend it we may be quite sure that the music of what we may call the "classical" Russian masters would be of as little interest and importance to-day as Grieg's or Dvorák's, equally colourful and equally picturesque. Qualities such as these may impress "the awakening intelligence of the musical masses," but they do not weigh very heavily with the cultured musician and fail altogether, therefore, to account for the tremendous influence of the Russians on so much of the Western European music written during the quarter of a century following Tchaïkovsky's death. These were not the qualities to impress such widely different spirits as Claude Debussy and Franz Liszt, the conservative Weingartner and the mercurial Beecham (to take only four names at random), and it is worth remarking that the one man who had no sounder elements than these in his make-up, and of whom Parry was chiefly thinking when he wrote the lines quoted, is the only important nineteenth century Russian composer whose position is weaker to-day than it was thirty years ago. Among the later men Scriabin, too, must be placed with Tchaïkovsky. Both, despite numerous affinities with their compatriots, are rather isolated figures and their most characteristic work remains outside the main current of Russian art.* This is not to be explained by

* Of all Russian musicians of the first rank, they are the only romantics. Their music is subjective, while all other Russian music of anything like the same value is curiously objective. But Tchaïkovsky, at any rate, was as *essentially* Russian as he was not *typically* Russian.

their attitude to conscious nationalism, with its borrowing and assimilating of folk-songs, for Tchaïkovsky, at any rate, was almost as fond of drawing on the great reservoir of peasant music as were any of the enthusiasts of the "mighty handful."* And neither Tchaïkovsky nor Scriabin was lacking in any of the colourful and emotional elements which Parry considered so characteristic of Russian music. We must go a little deeper than this, then, in our search for those qualities which are the real secret of our delight. The search for good qualities will bring to light the bad and indifferent ones at the same time, and so gradually we shall disengage the peculiarities which distinguish the Russian musical mentality so sharply from that of any of the Western peoples.

Perhaps the most valuable of all the qualities of Russian music is its compressed force and directness of expression. Its permanent intellectual appeal is almost certainly due chiefly to this conciseness. While German music has for many years, until quite recently, tended to become more and more prolix, the Russians have always been remark-

*"Moguchaya kuchka" is usually translated "the invincible band." But "mighty handful" is a closer equivalent to the playful Russian nickname.

able for their pointed, forceful brevity. Even Wagner and Brahms are scarcely remarkable for the simplicity and economy of their utterance, while lesser men, earnest advocates like Bruckner and Mahler, with cases of real interest to present, frequently have to be turned out of court as intolerable bores. On the other hand, if we have any complaint to make of Russian music it is usually that it is too nakedly direct, too primitive, or too sketchy. But there can be no doubt as to which is the less objectionable weakness. We may not care a snap for Mussorgsky's realism and we may be rather irritated by his continual manifestations of technical clumsiness, but there can be no contesting the breath-taking mastery of dozens of pages of "Boris" and the songs, where some subtle emotion or some intensely dramatic situation is caught up and presented to us in terms of music with astounding force and simplicity. The slightest inflection of the vocal line—and that line scarcely ever anything more than speech made musical—the sketchiest of accompaniments, and Mussorgsky has cut the heart out of some little village tragedy and brought it home to us with startling power. Think, too, of the remarkable presentation of Boris's anguish in the "Duma" scene. From the same type of mind working in the field of symphonic composition was born such a short pithy saying, like a blow straight from the shoulder, as the opening theme of Borodin's Second Symphony:—

Ex. I

or the unison passage at the beginning of "Scheherazade," the "Schariar" theme which serves as a motto to the whole work. As early as Glinka (to whom, by the way, Parry's words scarcely apply at all) this conciseness was a striking characteristic of Russian music. His "Kamarinskaya" is splendidly to the point, and in listening to the "Ruslan and Lyudmila" Overture one is forcibly reminded of the phrase in which Bülow is said to have conveyed his impression of Berlioz's "Corsair"—"terse as a pistol shot." Even Scriabin, whatever his practice in his symphonic works, knew how to be economical in his shorter ones; many of his piano pieces are tiny masterpieces of compression, comparable only with some of Heine's lyrics.

But it is in the manner of handling the very fabric of music, and even more in the sources of inspiration, that we find men like Tchaïkovsky, Scriabin and Rachmaninov ranging themselves with Western musicians rather than with their compatriots. The impulse to create, the "jog" of inspiration, comes to all men in all countries from more or less the same sorts of things; differences in the results are usually caused by the way in which men react to the jog. It was merely because they were very self-conscious on one particular point that the Russian "nationalists" so branded themselves. Wagner, who in his way was quite as much a nationalist as any Balakirev or Rimsky-Korsakov, was self-conscious of another side of his genius—which he paraded in a similar way. But it *is* rather remarkable that hardly any of the best Russian music is inspired by erotic emotion, and less still by psychological self-analysis—commodities in which Scriabin and Tchaïkovsky, in common with the majority of Western composers, deal rather heavily. No musician has ever been a keener analyst of the human soul than Mussorgsky, but he never takes himself as his subject and his analysis is as impartial and objective as Flaubert's. Here, not for the last time, we may pause to notice a certain constancy in the working of the Russian mind in the very different spheres of music and literature. The two greatest masters of the Russian novel, Tolstoy and Dostoevsky, both intensely introspective as men, preserved almost complete detachment as artists; they were capable of drawing even themselves objectively!

In this absence of emotional appeal as in so much else, Glinka's work is the prototype. The "love interest" in "A Life for the Tsar" is as obviously manufactured as the same element in popular detective fiction, and is responsible for the worst pages of the score, just as the love-music of "Prince Igor" is the weakest part of that magnificent work. Love plays an even less important rôle in "Boris," and a merely secondary part in "Khovanshchina." In "The Golden Cockerel" it is burlesqued as Stravinsky burlesques it in "Petrushka." Surely no other artists have been so little inspired by *das Ewig-Weibliche!* When they are unable to scamp the "love-interest" altogether, Russian musicians —including even Tchaïkovsky in his stage-works as a whole—provide it perfunctorily. Except in the works of that most personal of artists, Scriabin, there is nothing in the least equivalent to "Tristan," the erotic side of Chopin, or the "Dichterliebe" in the whole range of Russian music. Indeed emotional expression of any sort is rather conspicuously lacking in Russian art. If emotion is present at all, it is usually rather curtly restrained. Patriotism, though seldom jingoism, comes fairly often to the fore, humour not infrequently, and a quick reaction to any suggestion of the grotesque is noticeable. But the excitement which Russian music manifests —and I use the word "manifests" advisedly, instead of "expresses"—is almost always physical, a direct glorification of animal joy of living and of brute strength, rather than spiritual. It is not on this account less intellectual, as might seem at first thought—but the intellectual appeal must be considered separately. Yet before we leave the emotional aspect of Russian music it is worth pointing out that the climaxes in nearly all the most remarkable symphonic works, our two notable exceptions again helping to prove the rule, are of purely musical and intellectual contrivance (for instance, the finale of "The Fire Bird") and do not arise from any emotional intensification. As the American critic, Paul Rosenfeld, says of those in "Scheherazade," they are "purely voluntary . . . . nothing other than the arbitrary thickening and distention of certain ideas."

Though Russian music differs to this extent from Western as regards emotional basis, the difference is as nothing compared with the difference in what I can only call "musical intellectuality." For real intellectual understanding of Russian music one almost needs an entirely new set of postulates. The Russian musical mind is essentially so naïve, naïve even in ingenuity. It is childlike in many other respects than its love for bright primary orchestral colours and its pure sensuous delight in sound for sound's sake. Its freedom from preconceptions opens the way to all sorts of curious triumphs. Borodin, for instance, unhampered by tradition, was able to write the scherzo of his Third Symphony in genuine quintuple time :—

Ex. 2.

while the more sophisticated Chopin, trying to move in the same measure (third movement of his C minor Sonata), stumbles about uneasily in a compound duple-plus-triple time. Sometimes the extreme primitiveness of outlook gives us a ruder shock. The Russian, for one thing, seems usually to be over-concerned with the thrill of the present moment in sound;* his mental vision is not sufficiently broad and retentive to get that pleasure which we derive from Brahms and Beethoven at their best, when we feel that, in Pater's phrase, the composer has "foreseen the end in the beginning and never lost sight of it." Rimsky-Korsakov, in his "Record of my Musical Life," that most valuable (if not always completely reliable) of all original documents to the student of Russian music, tells us how in the eighteen-sixties the members of the "mighty handful" used to form their judgments. "For the most part a work was criticised by its separate elements; the first four bars were excellent, the next eight weak, the following melody was valueless, but the transition to the next phrase was good—and so on. A composition was never considered as an æsthetic whole. Accordingly Balakirev usually introduced new works to his circle fragmentarily; he used to play the end first, then the beginning . . . . "

Of the most typical Russians only Borodin, and Balakirev in his later years, seem to have been at all concerned with formal architecture in its

* Tchaïkovsky lives too intensely in this "present moment" *emotionally* as Rimsky-Korsakov does *sensuously*.

broadest aspect, Tchaïkovsky and Glazunov did their best to keep to the path of orthodoxy, with unhappy results in Tchaïkovsky's case, for the mechanical symmetry of the older type of symphony becomes ridiculous in works highly charged with emotion. Even Scriabin managed better than this. But with Rimsky-Korsakov the problems of form seem to have been confined entirely to the rough "lay-out" and general arrangement of ideas, that is, to mere "design" rather than to "form" in the true sense of the word. And he is not usually very deeply concerned with that. As for Stravinsky, his big ballets are, from a strictly musical point of view, literally incoherent as wholes. The unity of works like "Svadebka" ("Les Noces") is due to their peculiarly woven texture, a texture made by the kaleidoscopic rearrangement of tiny particles—a development of Rimsky-Korsakov's so-called "miniature style" in opera, which we shall have to consider later in more detail.

The basis of modern musical construction in Western Europe, the system of logical development of germinal ideas, of which Beethoven was the first really important master, is entirely foreign to the spirit of Russian music. There have been exceptions, of course; but, broadly speaking, the most typical Russian composers have either frankly abandoned the method or used it with conspicuous want of success. With the Russians we are never able to watch a few tiny germs unfold, showing themselves ever in new lights, till their possibilities seem almost inexhaustible and they have grown into a great and finely-wrought fabric of sound. Such thinking in sound—*progressive* thinking—is not the Russian's way of going about things; his mental process is more akin to brooding, a continual turning over of ideas in his mind, viewing them from different angles, throwing them against strange and fantastic backgrounds, but never *evolving* anything from them. We shall see one peculiarly Russian way of developing melody—by the insertion of appoggiaturas which are afterwards broadened to form an essential part of the line—when we come to examine "Prince Igor" a little more closely. And if we want modern examples of the same thing we shall find them again in "Svadebka." It is instructive, too, to compare the forward impulse of even a sustained Beethoven melody like "In des Lebens Frühlingstagen," in "Fidelio," with the static nature of the opening melody of "The Rite of Spring":—

Ex. 3.

It is almost like putting a Rodin against a Grecian frieze. And in this respect it is easy to find plenty of folk-song counterparts for the Stravinsky example.

When we turn to the field of opera this inability to think progressively, this mental trait of making the most of the subject by showing it passively in fresh circumstances instead of by setting it in active conflict with something else, produces even more curious results. Contrast and conflict, and through them progressive development, are the essence of drama, as we conceive it, just as they are the essence of sonata-form. The lack of them is far more obvious on the stage than in a symphonic movement, and though apparently a more serious defect—from our point of view—it has this advantage that it is the much more easily grasped. There can be no quibbling about the facts in opera; the presence or absence of this element of conflict is hardly demonstrable in pure music, but in opera it is so obvious that it needs no demonstration. In the finest and most characteristic Russian operas, "Igor," "Boris," "Sadko," even in the earliest of them all, "A Life for the Tsar," we find only the sketchiest outline of a plot, no drama of development, but a brilliant series of stage-pictures, sometimes highly dramatic in themselves, sometimes not at all so, detached and apparently almost disconnected yet cumulatively most effective in their presentation of an exuberantly vital whole. And it is significant that this is particularly true of the masterpieces, while some of the less important Russian operas—for instance, Rimsky-Korsakov's "Tsar's Bride" and "Pan Voevoda"—approach much more nearly the Western idea of theatrical effectiveness. It may be said that this is due simply to the composers' lack of stage-sense, but as it happens we only need turn to the work of non-musical dramatists to realise that this inability to see an action or a conflict of wills as the complete and rounded thing *we* call drama must spring from something deeply rooted in the Slav nature. Prince D. S. Mirsky has pointed out that "Tolstoy's dramatic method was not dramatic—his plays (as he has explained himself) are a succession of peep-show slides, rather than a dynamically unfolded action. So that a play by Tolstoy has more in common with a picture-series like 'The Rake's Progress' of Hogarth than with a real drama." Might not the same be said of Tolstoy's "War and Peace"? As for "Boris," Mussorgsky's opera is actually less diffuse than the play by Pushkin on which it is based.* The important thing is to remember that this lack of dramatic interest, a serious weakness in Western eyes, is no weakness to a Russian. He is aware of it, but it does not worry him. Rimsky-Korsakov himself described "Sadko" as an "opera-epic" consisting of "seven tableaux of a fabulous and epic nature."

In more purely musical matters—harmony, counterpoint and modulation—the working of the Russian mind differs quite as essentially from that of the Western. Harmonic thought is a personal

---

* Maurice Baring says of Pushkin's "Boris": "The play is constructed on the model of Shakespeare's chronicle plays, but in a still more disjointed fashion, without a definite beginning or end. . . . . Pushkin had not the power of conceiving and executing a drama which should move round one idea to an inevitable close. . . . . A subject from which a drama might be written is taken, but the drama is left unwritten. . . . It is not a play, but a chronicle; and it would be foolish to blame Pushkin for not accomplishing what he never attempted. As a chronicle, a series of detached scenes, it is supremely successful."

affair, at any rate in the case of a mature master. Many of Rimsky-Korsakov's harmonic idiosyncrasies, for instance, are peculiar to himself and certain harmonic progressions stamp a work as his quite as definitely as some of his favourite melodic shapes. But one can say without hesitation that, generally, harmony forms as inessential a part of a Russian composer's original conception as colour did of Brahms's.* To put it in another way: the bulk of Russian music is as clearly "harmonised" as Brahms's is "orchestrated." The music is conceived in terms of melody and colour; the harmony is a support, a filling-out, a spice—anything but a living organism. And much the same may be said of Russian counterpoint. Genuine contrapuntal feeling, the production of the musical texture by the natural flowing together of parallel, simultaneous streams of thought, is practically unknown in Russian music. On the other hand, some of the Russians have been very fond of using contrapuntal means in constructing their music, a fundamentally different matter. Borodin, in particular, frequently shows great ingenuity in juggling with combinations

* On the other hand, Tchaïkovsky told Mme. von Meck that "every melodic idea brings its own inevitable harmony."

BORODIN

of themes, but the themes (as in the well-known "On the Steppes of Central Asia") are only fitted together; they have not *grown* together. There is nothing forced or unnatural about the fitting, but the resulting musical texture is, as the composer himself, being a chemist, might have put it, a "mixture," not a "compound." Rimsky-Korsakov was another good theoretical contrapuntist; his Sextet, his String Quartet and his Third Symphony are monuments—one might almost say, tombstones—of academic counterpoint. But in his most characteristic works he never achieves anything like the living woof of parts which men like Wagner and Strauss manage so well. At its best, as in the magnificent finale of the fourth tableau of "Sadko," his counterpoint amounts to nothing more than ingenious dovetailing. More often it is a mere loose patchwork of themes like this example from "Scheherazade":—

Ex. 4.

Yet another typical idiosyncrasy of the Russian

musician is his habit of suddenly "pivoting" on one or two notes common to two chords, a sort of right-angled turn of thought which has either the piquant quality of an epigram or the disconcerting effect of a logical *non sequitur*, according to the skill with which it is managed. A simple, and very delightful, example is the trumpet fanfare which opens each part of "Tsar Saltan":—

Ex. 5.

There is a more elaborate one in the second movement of "Scheherazade":—

Ex. 6.

and it is characteristic of Rimsky-Korsakov that, having discovered this little trick of harmonic sleight-of-hand, he amuses himself with it at great length in sheer childish delight at the fun of the thing. The first time we hear it we accept it as a piece of genuine wit, wit being a matter of unexpected juxtapositions, but the joke becomes tiresome when the point is put in italics. The same trait shows itself in the general fondness for what we may call "enharmonic puns," not only as modulatory short cuts but for their own sakes. There is a startling instance in Balakirev's First Symphony, where, taking F sharp as G flat, he pivots suddenly from E minor to E flat minor, stays in the new key for four bars and then returns almost as abruptly.

One could multiply examples of similar tricks of musical thought almost indefinitely. Some, of course, are peculiar to individual composers, but many are common to practically all Russians and are the tokens of a far more essential "Russianness" than that which finds expression in the borrowing or imitation of folk-songs. The folk-song element is immensely important—both in symphonic music and in opera—but it offers no difficulty to the Western musical mind. Rather the reverse, for Russian folk-song is generally very attractive. It is the entire freshness of viewpoint—so delightful to anyone with an open mind—which has led to so much misunderstanding of Russian music on the part of those who put no very high value on its more superficial qualities. We are so accustomed to logical development in a symphony and to a particular kind of architecture in the drama that we have the greatest difficulty in appreciating any other ways of building a musical or theatrical fabric. We condemn as a "weakness" the absence of what we are accustomed to find, forgetting that it is as natural for a Russian to think episodically as for a Frenchman to think logically. There are plenty of real weaknesses in Russian music, as we soon find when we come to look more closely at individual works, but it is most important to distinguish between these and what are only peculiarly Russian ways of doing things. Mere freedom from prejudice is not enough; one must arm oneself with active will-to-understand. That need not preclude open-eyed criticism.

II.—GLINKA AND HIS ACHIEVEMENT.

SOME knowledge of the conditions under which work is produced must obviously be helpful, if not essential, to its complete understanding in any circumstances, but in few cases is it so absolutely necessary as in Glinka's. Only with the fullest realisation of his environment can one estimate with justice the extent of his achievement; that is, of his achievement considered positively as a thing valuable in itself, as apart from the value of its influence in determining the direction and methods of the later nationalist movement. One can talk glibly enough about this latter aspect of Glinka's work without even troubling to make its acquaintance, for his name has long since become petrified into a landmark of musical history. We perfunctorily touch our hats to it in passing and do not bother to examine it more closely.

In the case of the average composer, education, social position, immediate intellectual environment and the general state of national culture certainly modify his work, but they can scarcely be said actually to condition it, to define and limit it on all sides. Yet this was so with Glinka. Indeed, one may go further and say that the force of surrounding circumstances was a generating as well as a controlling one. Glinka was no Beethoven or Wagner imposing himself on circumstances, moulding them to his will and hacking a way through difficulties. Nor was he a Bach, a Mozart or a Haydn mutely accepting conditions as he found them, yet working such miracles within those limits that one is unconscious of them. His part was almost a passive one. His enthusiasms were like those of any dilettante and his triumphs of real artistic insight seem to be lucky hits rather than fruits of harnessed inspiration. A wealthy amateur, amiable, modest, gifted, highly strung (as witness Lenz's well-known anecdote of his behaviour on hearing the Choral Symphony),* almost always ill, either in fact or in imagination, playing the violin indifferently well and the piano better, as became a pupil of Field and Charles Mayer, dabbling in composition, though with the

---

* In "Beethoven et ses trois styles," and quoted by Grove ("Beethoven and his Nine Symphonies," p. 362).

scantiest technical equipment, his only serious, systematic study of the technique of composition was made in the five months he spent with Siegfried Dehn in Berlin in 1833, when he was twenty-nine—and twenty-three years later, the year before his death, he went back to Dehn and studied "Das Wohltemperirte Klavier." Yet this rather simple-minded avoider of unpleasant sensations was the initiator of a movement which exercised a fertilising influence on music during the last century second in importance only to that of Wagner himself. One can hardly say that he was unconscious of what he was doing, but his consciousness was much less definite than that of his immediate followers. As Fouque remarks, "It was only after his death that he became a reformer and innovator; in his life-time his ambition was not so far-reaching." Of ambition he had, indeed, as little as any creative artist can have. From such a man it is obvious that no great personal message could have come. His music is as nearly impersonal as music can be. The light which shines through it scarcely ever comes from his own rather colourless personality but is generated by the excitement of external circumstances. It is to the force of these surrounding influences that we owe alike the power, the colour and the weakness of Glinka's art. From the days of the pampered, coddled childhood to the journey to Italy made in 1830, nothing occurred to lay bare the real artist concealed beneath the dilettante exterior. His education completed, there was nothing for him to do but to write variations for harp and piano, to fall mildly in love and to travel for health's sake in the Ukraine and the Caucasian provinces. At home, at Novospasskoe, he certainly gained useful knowledge both of the orchestral classics and of the mechanism of the instruments from a little band kept by a wealthy uncle and, beside a number of trifles, he even produced a cantata for the accession of Nicholas I, of which he speaks complacently in his memoirs. But of exceptional gifts there was yet no sign. At St. Petersburg where, as in cultured circles all over Europe at that time, Italian opera was at the height of its glory, "he plunged for some time into a half-artistic, half-worldly life among a number of wealthy young fellows of good birth, fond of fêtes and serenades and theatrical performances."*

It was the long holiday in Italy (1830-1833) and

* M. D. Calvocoressi: "Glinka: biographie critique."

the consequent home-sickness which revealed the real Glinka, even to himself. The brilliant superficialities of Bellini and Donizetti repelled him at the same time that they fascinated him, and although they left marks on his style which he could never quite remove they now irritated his nostalgic melancholy. In this mood was born the resolve to "write music in Russian" and it was not long before opera suggested itself as the medium. Then came the five months with Dehn in Berlin, and by the time he reached home again he had already composed fragments of what was later to be "A Life for the Tsar," though, curiously enough, he had as yet a different subject in mind. Even when the new subject was suggested to him by Zhukovsky, his musical thought was independent of any consideration but the broad outline of the drama; at times he was actually in advance of the librettist (Rosen, the German secretary of the Tsarevich). Nothing could prove more clearly the absolutely musical genesis of "A Life for the Tsar"—though, musically, the progenitors of the work were an ill-assorted couple, Italian opera and Russian folk-song, the one the environment of his childhood, the other that of his maturer years. Yet the thing succeeded.

The first performance was on November 27 (December 9), 1836, and the success was both immediate and lasting. Only a few aristocrats sneered at the "coachman's music." But the Tsar was favourable, accepted the dedication, nominated the composer Master of the Imperial Chapel, and hailed Glinka as "a great master." Encouraged by this initial triumph, Glinka now turned to Pushkin's "Ruslan and Lyudmila" for a new libretto and, but for the author's tragic death, might have had his assistance in redrafting the work for a musical setting. He worked at "Ruslan" from 1837 to 1842, producing also the incidental music to Kukolnik's tragedy, "Prince Kholmsky," during the same period. Calvocoressi remarks that this is to be considered the period during which the composer's artistic development reached maturity and that not only is "Ruslan" incomparably finer than "A Life for the Tsar," but in itself shows a great advance on its first sketches. Such an advance has quite a different significance in Glinka's case from that which, thanks to Nottebohm, we can trace in the development of many of Beethoven's ideas. With Beethoven it shows only the operation of the technical process of refinement; with Glinka it is the token of the composer's increasingly sure grip on his whole means of expression. Yet "Ruslan," much farther removed from Italianism than "A Life for the Tsar," had only a moderate success and Glinka, discouraged, wrote no more for six years.

To opera he never returned. The output of his later years consists entirely of those "picturesque fantasias" with which he hoped to please "equally the connoisseurs and the general public," compromises between "the exigencies of art and those of the time," to use the composer's own words.* The material for two of these, the "Capriccio on the Jota Aragonesa" and "Summer Night in Madrid," was provided by the realisation of a "far-off dream of youth," a visit to Spain (1845-47), in the course of which he made considerable, if not very scientific, researches into the nature and origin of Spanish folk-music. He was particularly struck by the Oriental flavour of much of it—attributable apparently to Moorish elements. In 1848 we find him again in Warsaw after a brief stay at home. Here he wrote another of his orchestral fantasias, the well-known "Kamarinskaya," based on two Russian folk-tunes, one of which he had already turned to

* Letter to Kukolnik.

account in a piano piece. Again in 1852 his love of travel led him through Berlin and Paris to the south of France and then back to Paris, where he composed a fragment of a "Ukrainian Symphony." This was a programmatic work based on Gogol's "Taras Bulba," but it was soon abandoned on account of "the impossibilty of getting out of the German rut in the development"—significant phrase and explanatory of what many would take for weaknesses in Glinka's work. This fragment really marks the end of Glinka's creative career, if career it can be called, though he wrote an orchestral polonaise for the coronation of Tsar Alexander II in 1855. Glinka had been driven home by the outbreak of the Crimean War and, except for the Berlin visit of 1856, spent the last three years of his life in complete quiet. He studied church music and toyed with a new libretto but, though still a middle-aged man, he did not rouse himself to any creative effort. It was at this time that he met the critic-composer Serov and Alexander Dargomïzhsky, who without Glinka's richer qualities was yet able to accomplish those reforms in the nature of Russian opera in which the other had only partly succeeded. And then there was the young Balakirev (introduced to him by that Ulibishev whom we remember chiefly as an authority on Mozart and as the antagonist of von Lenz as a Beethoven critic), Balakirev who was to become the leader of that "mighty handful" who soon trod Glinka's little footpath into a broad and noble road. Glinka recognised the boy of nineteen as his natural successor: "He alone has ideas so like my own about everything concerned with music . . . . In time he will be the second Glinka."

For all critical purposes Glinka's work may be considered as consisting only of the two operas, the "Prince Kholmsky" music and the orchestral fantasias. With the exception of one or two effective songs, such as Chaliapin's favourite battle-steed, "The Midnight Review," and one or two *salon* pieces for piano, the remainder of his output "does not even," as Calvocoressi says, "reveal a temperament." Such a handful of works, for none of which (except "Ruslan") any but the most enthusiastic admirer* could claim artistic perfection, extraordinary beauty or very uncommon imaginative power, seems to offer but small ground on which to

* There have been many such in Russia, however—Tchaïkovsky, Anton Rubinstein and Rimsky-Korsakov among the rest.

build any substantial claim for respecting Glinka as anything but a pioneer. Yet I should like to show if I can that Glinka deserves admiration for something more than the fact of his being the first to "write Russian music," that, within the limits imposed on him by the special conditions I have outlined, he produced some really remarkable work and that this work is, in any case, specially worthy of study on account of those unique conditions. By far the most interesting and important of these is Glinka's technical "incompetence."

It is easy enough to laugh at his awkward modulations and his naïve solutions of the problems of symphonic architecture—and to miss the point completely. After all, how otherwise could he have managed things? This Russian musical language had to grow from itself, or rather (if I may mix metaphors) to form its own channel. Traditional methods would have corrupted the purity of the young growth and perhaps even stifled it altogether. Better almost any weaknesses and severe growing pains than that. Glinka himself recognised this very clearly; "Taras Bulba" was thrown over because of "the impossibility of getting out of the German rut," and elsewhere he says that "severe

German counterpoint is not always in accord with imaginative fire." It is easy to say that his was a short-sighted view, that he ignored the fact that "those move easiest who have learn'd to dance." But surely he was right in preferring natural awkwardness to the dancing-master correctness of deportment of the academic product who says next to nothing in the nicest possible way. Learning is like fuel; it feeds the fire, yet too much will put it out. Too much counterpoint nearly extinguished Rimsky-Korsakov and the same accident might have befallen Glinka. On the other hand, given something new and vital to express, that something will, in spite of every disadvantage, find a natural outlet through which to express itself. (Your illiterate tinker of Bedford will, in his earnestness, turn you out noble prose, while the Great Cham of English literary scholarship could write only a laboured jargon.) So we may imagine Glinka facing these rough ashlars of popular melody, feeling instinctively that there must be some way of hewing them into fine and vital shapes. The tools that every craftsman uses are ready to his hand, but they are designed to work in other material than this, even if he could use them less awkwardly. So he struggles—and sometimes flounders helplessly enough—as every man must struggle who sets out to make something in a new way, without model or precedent and without the skill of the long-practised craftsman. Hence the loose, almost amorphous designs of the symphonic fantasias, for instance, "A Summer Night in Madrid," in which one theme is merely taken up after another, without coherence, till at the very end the two most important are picked up again and brilliantly dismissed in the brief coda. Only the fleeting later references to the "Punto Moruno" tune show that the composer is aiming at anything more organic than a piece of patchwork. The "Capriccio on the Jota Aragonesa" hangs together better only because of the economy of material. But it is in "Kamarinskaya," the most interesting in every way, that the difficulty of spinning a more or less sophisticated art-work out of popular material is displayed most clearly and grappled with, if by no means solved, most successfully. Here, more truly than anywhere else in Glinka, we may say that the form has grown round the substance and "corresponds to the real nature and purport of it." It is admittedly crude and amateurish but, despite its looseness, it is in this respect a more notable achievement than the "Ruslan" Overture. The Overture, by far the best thing Glinka ever wrote on classical lines, is concise, well organised, bearing no marks of technical incompetence, and giving an impression of striking vigour and confidence, even of great power (in the famous passage near the end where the trombones play a descending whole-tone scale *fortissimo*):—

Ex. 7.

The problem of fitting the material into a given design is satisfactorily solved, but one can hardly say that the form has arisen naturally from the material or is conditioned by it in any way. But "Kamarinskaya" is a natural growth.

"Kamarinskaya" also raises, and to some extent answers, a question of fundamental principle in the treatment of folk-song material in sophisticated music. We must remember what a folk-song is—and how much it is that. A man's music is the manifestation of a something which is the sum of many things—thoughts, emotions, and purely musical feelings and ideas. In the music of a competent composer that "something," complicated as it may be, is expressed more or less completely and satisfactorily; in folk-music, although the "something" is usually simple, it frequently is not. In the majority of cases a folk-tune, divorced from the words, gives only an imperfect idea of the spirit of which it is the outward manifestation. Its beauty is the beauty of a body without a soul, which is perhaps the explanation of its peculiar charm. When he sets such a tune a composer may be content merely to dress up the body to the best advantage or he may try to breathe into it again the spirit which gave it life in the first place. To do the first skilfully is good and useful work, but craftsman-work; the artist can be content with nothing less than a re-creation of the vital spirit. To take familiar examples: this is precisely what Delius has done in "Brigg Fair" and what Grainger has failed to do in his choral setting of the same tune, true and beautiful though his treatment is.

Now this is what Glinka attempted, but did not quite achieve, in "Kamarinskaya," if not in the two

Spanish fantasias. He failed—or only partially succeeded—because his material was not thoroughly digested. It was not seen through a personality, as the "Brigg Fair" tune is seen through Delius's, and so the easiest way of recreating the feeling at the back of the thing was missed. Time after time we do realise the dim presence of the real soul re-created, only to be baffled again by patches of what is only a brilliantly scored "setting" of the tune. Even so, it is far in advance of its time—in advance, too, of the methods of the Smetanas and Liszts and Griegs and Dvoraks of later years.*

For Glinka had the root of the matter in him. He had the right method of approach, realisation of the fundamental fact that what folk-melody needs, if it is to be used in art-music, is to be displayed against fresh backgrounds. That is to say, the tune, in whatever fresh lights and relationships it may be shown, must not be mangled by subjecting it to the largely mechanical processes of "development"

* Tchaïkovsky thought "Kamarinskaya" "astonishingly original," and said that "from it all the Russian composers who followed Glinka (including myself) continue to this day to borrow contrapuntal and harmonic combinations directly they have to develop a Russian dance-tune. . . . . Glinka managed to concentrate in one short work what a dozen second-rate talents would only have invented with the entire expenditure of their powers."

which have been devised to exploit quite a different kind of material. The method of "fresh back-grounds" is peculiarly congenial to the Russian mind and was long employed exclusively by the Russians, but as a formula for folk-song treatment it is popular with modern composers of every nationality. (Among the latter one may be pardoned for referring once more to Delius, and incidentally for pointing out the curious parallel between his social position and haphazard manner of drifting into the world of music and Glinka's.) Perhaps the most serious objection to Glinka's method is the glaring light it throws on the poverty of a composer's inventive resources and on any weaknesses in the material. Glinka nowhere works with really first-rate material, but whether here in "Kamarinskaya," where it is quite weak :—

Ex. 8.

in the Spanish "Capriccio," or in the best pages of "Ruslan" (for instance, the chorus that opens Act III and the splendid dances of Act IV), he is seldom at a loss for ideas for original and often daring treatment. This is particularly noticeable in the "Ruslan" dances.

It will perhaps be objected that Glinka, for all his care in avoiding the Charybdis of German thought and methods, crashed heedlessly on to the Scylla of Italianism in opera—apparently the worse evil. This is true, above all, of "A Life for the Tsar." But since it was almost inevitable that at first some foreign matter should mingle with the pure metal, it was really fortunate that the other component should be Italian rather than German, seeing that the former was far easier to eliminate afterwards. And though Glinka never entirely threw off this weakening influence, its power over him was at its worst confined almost entirely to manner and method. His essential thought was but little corrupted by it, and in the crucible of his mind the very clichés of the Italians became as Russianised as the Spanish tunes in the "Summer Night in Madrid." When, as in Finn's and Ruslan's songs in the Second Act of "Ruslan," both thought and expression are altogether native, the result is strikingly fine. The march in the "Prince Kholmsky" music is an instance of a triumph over, or rather *through*, another kind of commonplace. Naîve and square-cut as it is, there is a certain dignity in its rude strength and it admirably expresses what it is intended to express—an outburst of popular feeling at a national crisis. Glinka is not to be compared with Mussorgsky or even Rimsky-Korsakov as an interpreter of mass-feeling, but, like so many Russian intellectuals, he drew power from his sympathy with the people. Even Mussorgsky never surpassed the "Slavsya" chorus in "A Life for the Tsar."

Glinka's strength—and one feels that it is never the man's own force of character, but some outward exciting circumstance that is the driving power—

Ex. 9.

nearly always finds expression in the roughest way. It is better controlled in the "Ruslan" Overture than in anything else he did. But it scarcely ever finds an outlet in those barbaric outbursts to which Russian orchestral music owes so much of its superficial attractiveness. Yet even of these we get a foretaste in the *lezginka* of "Ruslan" and the Prelude to Act V of "Prince Kholmsky" (Ex. 9). One gets a keener thrill of sensuous pleasure from this than from most of Glinka's work, but the naïve, healthy vigour of almost all the things really worthy of him is extremely refreshing. The thought is always simple, usually individual (though not, as I have tried to show, very personal) and often extremely beautiful. And though its expression is not always completely free, it is probably little more hampered by the medium than is the essential thought of many composers of far greater reputation. After all the number of composers who have entirely subdued their means of expression to the supple instrument of their thought, to the natural ease of a limb rather than of a skilfully handled tool, is surprisingly small.

Glinka, of course, was often clumsy enough in quite elementary matters of craftsmanship. To the end he remained too much the dilettante to master the tricks that every Mus.Doc. in England has at his fingr-tips. But in one branch of workmanship he was always conspicuously successful and his mastery is overlooked only because of the still more remarkable triumphs of his younger fellow-countrymen in the same line. As an orchestrator he deserves a very high place indeed. In his attitude to the orchestra, as in his treatment of folk-song in "Kamarinskaya," Glinka is very nearly abreast of the composer of the present day, in that the instrumental colour forms an essential part of his original conception. Though Glinka never arrived at that point where the exigencies of instrumental colour begin to influence the line itself one never feels, as one does with nearly all his Western contemporaries, that the colour is merely a more or less happy afterthought. To whatever source he owed it, the experiments with his uncle's little orchestra or the contact with Berlioz (only made, however, when "Ruslan" was finished), his sureness of touch was remarkable. As the French master himself wrote in the "Journal des Débats," Glinka handled the instruments "with understanding of their most secret resources." Rimsky-Korsakov never tired of singing the praises of Glinka's "enchanting scoring" and its "lightness and transparency." His own style of orchestration was for many years deliberately modelled on Glinka's; right up to 1888, that is until after the composition of "Scheherazade," the "Capriccio Espagnol" and the "Easter Festival" Overture, his method of scoring was simply a development of Glinka's. It was only after the "Ring" performances in St. Petersburg in the winter of that year, that he came under Wagner's influence. It is easy to see how the percussion writing in the "Capriccio" and "Scheherazade" is modelled on that in "A Summer Night in Madrid," but the similarity of orchestral handling goes much deeper than that.

One hardly knows which to admire the more in Glinka, his mastery of the orchestral palette as a whole or his treatment of the individual instruments. In both the Spanish fantasias the handling of the broad masses of colour is exceedingly rich and brilliant; "Kamarinskaya," less rich, has a hard, transparent brilliance of its own. The clarinet solo in the latter work is perfectly suited to the instrument and the clarinet is again treated with fine insight in "Ruslan." One passage in particular is so essentially "clarinettish" that I must qualify my observation that Glinka "never" derived his melodic line from the nature of an instrument:—

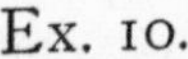
Ex. 10.

But to point out little technical points of this kind would lead one into a boundless wilderness of praise. One can only mention their presence as some sort of compensation for the awkward harmonies and floundering modulations which offend the ear accustomed to a more polished style of utterance.

III.—THE FOLK-SONG ELEMENT.

THE problem of the use of folk-song material in symphonic music presented itself to Glinka's successors in a different and more difficult form than it had done to Glinka himself. He had been concerned with nothing more than the stringing together of folk-tunes into frankly popular fantasias, harmonising them and orchestrating them so as to complete the spiritual pictures for which they were only rough sketches. Dargomïzhsky, in his "Fantasia on Finnish Themes," and the young Balakirev, in his "Overture on Three Russian Themes," seem to have been content to do no more. But as the younger Russians developed, these rather naïve forms no longer satisfied them. They began to write more elaborate orchestral compositions still very largely based on folk-melodies, and found themselves faced with the extraordinary difficulty of fusing into the most complicated of musical organisms—sonata-form on the symphonic scale—the simplest of all natural forms of musical organism. For a folk-song is a complete entity, not a mere cell as a motif is, and therein lies the difficulty. Being already a fully developed whole, it contains no growing power. Nor, without vandalism, can it be decomposed into its constituent parts and these parts treated as germ-cells. Glinka's instinct in rejecting conventional development was sound, but his successors found it almost impossible to go further than he had done without it.

Of course, when we speak of particular artistic "problems" and "difficulties" we do not necessarily imply that the artists themselves were specially conscious of them. Rimsky-Korsakov and Tchaïkovsky and the rest of them were probably quite unaware how their problem differed from Glinka's. There is no reason to suppose that they were aware of a definite "problem" at all; it was simply that they admired these melodies and wanted to weave them into their compositions. They were still obsessed with the idea that, as Glinka had put it, "the people were the composers; *they* were only the arrangers." But the problem, akin to that of the novelist who borrows characters from history, existed all the same and we can get a great deal of insight into each composer's mind if we can see how he solved it.

The composer's difficulties begin even in such an apparently simple matter as the harmonisation of a folk-tune. The ideal method, no doubt, would be to employ only such harmonies as are implied by the melodic line; but, like so many ideals, it is hardly practicable or even desirable. The way of the purist is seldom that of the creative artist; he finds more congenial society among critics. But one can sympathise with Rimsky-Korsakov's anxiety about the harmonisation of his two well-known collections, the "Hundred Russian Folk-Songs," Op. 24, and the smaller collection of forty songs taken down from the singing of T. I. Filippov. He continually remodelled his settings before he was satisfied that his harmonisations were "simple and Russian enough." Yet for all his pains, he was not preserving the purity of peasant art as he imagined, for like Balakirev, Lyadov and all the other supposedly "sympathetic" folk-song arrangers of his circle, he was on a wrong scent altogether. Their fundamentally wrong conception of Russian folk-music as homophonic was pointed out in their own lifetime by Y. N. Melgunov, who died as long ago as 1893, but his discovery of the polyphonic nature of a great deal of Russian folk-music came just too late to influence the development of Russian art-music.* In the whole of the Russian classics there is only one genuine example of folk-harmony—the unaccompanied peasants' chorus in the last act of "Prince Igor." In its simplest form this folk-polyphony is produced by "under voices" *(podgoloski)* branching out from the chief melody, after an opening usually in unison, and rejoining it in the final cadence. But in many songs the polyphony has in the course of time become more and more elaborate, often producing bold and interesting harmonies. How completely this true folk-harmony differs from the harmonic idiom of the most sympathetic arrangers of the last century has been graphically shown by A. D. Kastalsky in his "Peculiarities of the Russian Folk Music System," in which he gives parallel examples of folk-harmonisations collected by Melgunov and Palchikov and harmonisations of the same melodies by

---

* The first part of his "Russian Songs" appeared in 1879, the second in 1885—and Rimsky-Korsakov condemned them as "barbarous"!

Glinka, Lyadov, Mussorgsky, Balakirev, Rimsky-Korsakov and Tchaïkovsky.*

This point is not very important. It is of no consequence that these composers harmonised folk-melodies in their own way when they used them in their own compositions. They were artists, not archæologists. But it does dispose once and for all of the commonly held view that the "Kuchkisti" and their followers knew very much more about peasant music than Tchaïkovsky did and treated it in a very different spirit. As a matter of fact, even in points of notation, he and they constantly tended to think along the same lines. In the familiar *andante cantabile* of his first String Quartet, for instance, Tchaïkovsky has written out the melody, "Sidel Vanya," with a key-signature of two flats as if it were in B flat major, although it is clearly in the mixolydian mode (i.e., in F, but with the E flattened). At the same time he has harmonised it throughout in the normal F major, with E natural. It might be said that he has not been very "sympathetic." Yet when Rimsky-Korsakov included the song in his "Hundred Folk-

* Some of these were reproduced in Victor Belaev's article on Kastalsky in "Music and Letters," Vol. X, No. 4.

Songs," five or six years later, his so-called arrangement consisted simply of a trifling modification of Tchaïkovsky's treatment of the tune when it returns later in the movement on the three upper strings in unison, though he omitted to acknowledge his obligation clearly in a foot-note. And although he thought it necessary to alter Tchaïkovsky's time-notation from four bars (2/4, 2/4, 3/4, 2/4) to two (4/4, 5/4), he adopted his key-notation, a much more important matter, just as it stands. In fact, Tchaïkovsky's bass is just such as Glinka might have written. It is only when we study his bigger (and later) orchestral works that we begin to see what differentiates Tchaïkovsky from the avowed nationalists.

It is particularly interesting to compare the treatment of the same tune by different composers; for example, Balakirev's handling of the song, "Vo pole bereza stoyala" ("In the plain stood a birch-tree") in his B minor "Overture on Three Russian Themes," with Tchaïkovsky's in the finale of his F minor Symphony, or Rimsky-Korsakov's use of a certain dance-tune from the Nizhny-Novgorod Government in *his* "Overture on Russian Themes" with Tchaïkovsky's in "1812." Such comparison

TCHAÏKOVSKY.

is not easy. We have to take into account the fact that the Balakirev Overture was written in 1858, the year after Glinka's death, by a twenty-one year old composer, while the Tchaïkovsky Symphony was composed nineteen years later by a man of thirty-seven. And we have to guard against facile generalisations suggested by knowledge derived from outside sources—saying, for instance, that Balakirev tries to identify himself with the popular spirit of the tune, while Tchaïkovsky only treats it as the symbol of something of which he remains a detached, if not unsympathetic, observer. That is true enough, but it has little or nothing to do with the purely musical treatment of the melody. When we come to examine that we can hardly avoid being struck more by the resemblances than by the differences. Tchaïkovsky uses a more primitive form of the tune, in which each of the two short phrases is exactly repeated, while Balakirev prefers one in which the repeated phrase is varied (the version given by Rimsky-Korsakov in his Op. 24). Balakirev, Rimsky-Korsakov and Tchaïkovsky agree in giving the melody a pedal bass. Balakirev treats the theme sometimes in close imitation, sometimes with creeping chromatic counter-themes; sometimes he intersperses it with rushing passage-work. Tchaïkovsky does all three. Tchaïkovsky, it may be objected, also uses the tune in diminution, distorting it in the "German manner" of development which Glinka had set his face against. But Balakirev's Overture opens with a passage in which precisely the same thing happens as in the working-out of Tchaïkovsky's finale; the theme in diminution is thrown quickly from one group of instruments to another and whirled into flights of rushing semiquaver octaves. Tchaïkovsky's "unsympathetic" treatment of the tune itself appears only in his obliteration of the three-bar rhythm and in the sensational showiness of the orchestration. Here Tchaïkovsky does seem to forget the origin of his material, to be thinkingof its possibilities as an occasion for orchestral fireworks in the abstract. (But Rimsky-Korsakov came nearer than he thought to doing the same thing in his "Easter Festival" Overture.) Yet after all, the impression we get that the "Birch Tree" tune is, so to speak, indigenous in the Balakirev piece but merely a foreign substance embedded in the Tchaïkovsky, is due more to the nature of the rest of the music than to the handling of the theme itself. Whereas in the Balakirev it is surrounded with music entirely based on other folk-material, in the Tchaïkovsky it is set in the middle of a good deal of gaudy stuff of the composer's own. Because Tchaïkovsky, despite his fairly numerous experiments with folk-music, never really absorbed its idiom, hardly even tinctured his style with it, he can never make his borrowings sound natural. When he quotes a folk-song the quotation never seems inevitable; it seldom matches his own ideas; it sounds as if it had been dragged in by the heels. He quotes like a headmaster showing off to the parents on a speech-day rather than like Elia.

When we turn to the attempts to grow symphonic music entirely from the seed of folk-song we have to leave Tchaïkovsky behind altogether. Cases like his Second Symphony and the finale of his popular String Serenade, Op. 48 (in which both the theme of the introduction and the principal subject of the *allegro con spirito* are folk-tunes), are quite exceptional in Tchaïkovsky's music. And even in these the subsidiary material is his own. He must have seen that these attempts of Balakirev and Rimsky-Korsakov were foredoomed to failure, or at any rate to failure directly they went beyond certain clearly defined limits. Indeed, when one considers the difficulty of the problem, it is astonishing that Balakirev and Korsakov achieved as much as they did either in quantity or quality. There is little to be said of Balakirev's early works, the overtures "on a Spanish March," "on Czech Themes," and the youthful B minor "on Russian Themes" already mentioned. They combine Glinka's methods with a surer mastery of musical architecture than Glinka showed. But in spite of their clearness of outline they remain essentially "fantasias." The themes are delightfully treated but they do not take root in the composer's mind and grow. The symphonic poem, "A Thousand Years," composed in 1862 to commemorate the tenth centenary of the foundation of the Russian state by Rurik, reorchestrated in 1887 and published under the title, "Russia," is on a different level. The three folk-tunes which provide the whole of the material (Nos. 1, 2 and 22 of Balakirev's own folk-song collection) are intended to symbolise "the three principal elements of our history: paganism, the Muscovite state, and the quasi-democracy of ancient Russia," and the struggle between these elements, terminated by Peter the

Great's "Westernising" reforms (which Balakirev, as a Slavophile, regarded as a national disaster), is supposed to be depicted in what the composer himself called an "instrumental drama." Actually the musical form and substance of "Russia" are much more like those of the earlier B minor Overture than a Lisztian symphonic poem. In essence it is glorified Glinka. It is certainly not programme-music in the usual sense of the word. Its superiority to the B minor Overture is due simply to the extraordinary quality of the musical imagination playing on the material. It towers above all other fantasias and overtures on Russian folk-themes not because the given melodies are handled with greater technical skill or because the composer has used them to a definite end, but because they clearly fired his imagination as another composer's imagination might have been fired by the act of conceiving themes of his own. Balakirev has *made* these his own by right of artistic conquest. Though almost every bar of the piece is based directly on the material (and there is hardly any conventional development) one completely forgets that the composer is "treating" themes. The process has altogether ceased to be an external one; it is the spontaneous chemistry of a creative mind working freely on perfectly congenial ideas. "Russia" is just as much "inspired" as if Balakirev had invented his own themes instead of borrowing them. It demonstrates beyond cavil what can be done wlth folk-material by a composer of genius. But it stands alone.

Of Balakirev's circle only Rimsky-Korsakov attempted to emulate him in this field. And of his handful of works we may neglect the early "Fantasia on Serbian Themes," Op. 6, a clever attempt to make bricks without straw, the Piano Concerto, Op. 30, and the Fantasia for Violin and Orchestra, Op. 33, a loosely-put-together occasional piece, almost redeemed by the beauty of its chief subject. The well-known "Easter Festival" Overture, Op. 36, is certainly based on traditional church-melodies but it seems to belong to a different genre. Like the Spanish themes of the "Capriccio Espagnol," the liturgical melodies of the Overture give one the impression, despite the composer's intention, of being little more than a pretext for the unloosing of a riot of gorgeous orchestral colour. The early D major "Overture on Russian Themes" was frankly modelled on Balakirev's B minor

Overture and "Russia," and may be ranked in achievement somewhere between these two works. It is a more effective piece of work than Balakirev's B minor but not to be compared with "Russia." Rimsky-Korsakov adopts Balakirev's plan without modification, an *allegro* on two themes with a slow introduction and coda based on a third, in this case, the familiar "Slava" melody used by Beethoven in the trio of the second "Razumovsky" Quartet and by Mussorgsky in the coronation scene of "Boris."* The opening theme of the *allegro* has been made equally well-known to Western audiences through Tchaïkovsky's "1812" Overture (the dance-tune in E flat minor). Though Rimsky-Korsakov's overture is dated 1880, when it was re-written and re-scored, and is numbered Op. 28, it was actually composed, and played at one of Balakirev's Free School Concerts, in 1866. It is therefore one of the earliest of all Rimsky-Korsakov's compositions and would have been more properly numbered Op. 2, Opus 1 being the First Symphony. The Sinfonietta, Op. 31, based on the first three movements of an unpublished string quartet written

* Rimsky-Korsakov also employed it again in a cantata, Op. 21, and as the leit-motif of Ivan the Terrible in "The Tsar's Bride."

in 1879, is a more important work, probably the biggest composition entirely based on folk-tunes ever written.* The first movement, autumnal in mood (it is based on a song, "Over the field creeps the mist"), is a particularly interesting attempt to solve this problem of folk-song treatment on symphonic lines. Roughly speaking it consists of a compromise between Glinka's methods and conventional development. There is development of a kind but, instead of a motif of three or four notes, two or four bars of melody are generally taken as the smallest unit. Balakirev had done something the same in his "Russia," but Korsakov's music is warmed by no corresponding play of imagination. He is more methodical; one can easily watch the working of his mind from bar to bar; and the themes are not very attractive. So an interesting point of view results in rather dull music. Again, the beautiful horn melody of the slow movement is spoiled by unimaginative harmonisation; at least, is spoiled for those who remember the simple harp chords with which Stravinsky supports the same tune in the *khorovod* of the captive princesses in "The Fire

* The score contains eight altogether, Nos. 12, 51, 68, 70, 75, 79 and 90 from his own Op. 24, and No. 31 of Balakirev's "Forty Russian Folk Songs."

Bird" or Rimsky-Korsakov's own arrangement of it in his Op. 24. Nor does the jolly, bustling scherzo-finale throw any fresh light on the problem. On the whole, then, Rimsky-Korsakov's essays in this field can be considered only moderately successful. He never digested the given material completely. It remained with him always some-

Ex. 11.

thing to be worked *on* rather than worked *with*. And so he was unlikely to hit on such a master-touch as the penultimate bar of Balakirev's "Russia," for instance. At the end of this poem the symbol of the old, pagan Russia creeps back on the lower strings, muted; the picture fades away in harp arpeggios; but the first violins float down, not to a final chord, but to die out into silence with a last fluttering reference to the chief theme* of the *allegro* (Ex. 11) surely one of the most imaginative endings in all music.

The only moral one can draw from "Russia" is the rather obvious one that success in the symphonic handling of folk-tunes is purely and simply a matter of genius corrected by good taste—"good taste" being shown here in the avoidance of virtuosity in the treatment of the material and in not making it an excuse for talking about oneself. But a genius capable of spinning a masterpiece from given material is far more likely to prefer to work with material of his own invention, which will not tie his hands at every turn by compelling him always to respect its original nature. It is significant that

* A melody which left its mark on a theme in Borodin's B minor Symphony (Ex. 26).

Balakirev used only one folk-theme (with a snatch of an Oriental melody) in his First Symphony (finished in 1898) and only two in his Second (completed ten years later). They are set out in a masterly way. In the context they sound like natural ebullitions of the composer's own high spirits. But he had definitely abandoned the ideas embodied in the overtures of forty years earlier, the attempt to create an instrumental art purely folkish in origin.

It is in the field of opera that folk-song has made its presence in Russian art-music most effectively felt. In opera folk-song no longer has to be self-sufficient. It finds itself in surroundings which support it, so to speak, and where it sounds more natural. The composer is no longer involved in a struggle to reconcile irreconcilables, the very simple and natural with the very complex and, in a sense, artificial. There is no temptation to develop something which by its nature obstinately refuses to develop, which is complete in itself and which cannot be subjected to ordinary symphonic methods without barbarously torturing it. Folk-song can be effectively turned to account in opera in half-a-dozen ways: as aria (Olga's "Stay with Me, my Love" in "Pskovityanka"), chorus (the last scene of

"Boris,"), leit-motif (Ivan the Terrible's theme in "The Tsar's Bride"), orchestral interlude (prelude to Act III of "Snegurochka") or ballet music (the "Cleopatra" scene of "Mlada"). It was a favourite device of Rimsky-Korsakov's to employ a folk-song sung by the chorus or in the orchestral accompaniment, as a background to dialogue-recitative. But on the whole the use of folk-song in Russian opera is more effective than interesting to the student. It gives a delightful flavour to the scores of the classical Russian masters, but throws no light on the composers themselves.

But in their operas, even more easily than in their symphonic music, we can trace their evolution of a natural folk-idiom of their own. If it is difficult to make up one's mind as to the æsthetic value of genuine folk-song as an element in art-music, it is twenty times more so in the case of imitated folk-song. It would appear at a first glance to be simpler; we are rid of borrowings; we no longer have to balance subtle differences of method of treatment; we do not need to consider whether a composer has been faithful to letter and spirit of an original, to decide whether or not he has done right in putting in or leaving out so much of himself, and so on. If the music is entirely his own we have to take into consideration nothing but its own merit. No doubt that *is* ultimately all that matters. But the difficulty is that folk-songish music, as distinct from genuine folk-music, is of two kinds, one perfectly natural, the other unpleasantly artificial—and that it is hardly possible to distinguish one from the other. Musical ideas naturally occur to a composer —or, as the romantic phrase has it, he is *inspired*— in terms of the musical idiom to which he is accustomed. If he is used to hearing tunes with certain well-marked tonal and melodic and rhythmical peculiarities, especially if he has heard a lot of them during the impressionable years of childhood, the themes which spontaneously occur to him will probably have the same peculiarities.* This, one feels sure, was what happened in Mussorgsky's case. He wrote in the folk-song idiom as naturally as Burns wrote in the Lowland Scottish dialect. The other essential elements of his musical

* This is more particularly likely to occur in his earlier work. He reproduces *with a difference,* and as he grows older he will, if he is a genuinely fertile composer, listen more and more to himself and less to outside influences. The maturing of a composer, the development of his musical personality, is probably nothing more than this—the reproduction of melodic, rhythmic and harmonic formulæ with ever greater modifications.

language were realistic, descriptive, imitative, expressionistic—anything but purely musical. Except a few altogether unimportant trifles,* the equivalents of Burns's unfortunate English poetry, everything Mussorgsky wrote is expressed in an idiom of which the only *musical* root is folk-song—however far, as for example in the clarinet melody at the end of "A Night on the Bare Mountain":—

Ex. 12.

it has grown from that root. Indeed Mussorgsky made the folk-idiom his own instrument so completely that it is rather easier to detect the quotation of an actual folk-melody in his music than in Rimsky-Korsakov's—which is less paradoxical than it at first seems to be.

The same, with modifications, may be said of Borodin. There were other elements in Borodin's

* "Il vecchio castello" in the "Exhibition Pictures" is the first example which springs to the mind, and is probably the best known.

musical make-up—reflected Schumann, reflected Balakirev, a natural oriental strain, and some remarkable streaks of absolute originality which give him a place apart. But in so far as he derives from Great Russian folk-music he seems to stand with Mussorgsky. But about Rimsky-Korsakov one cannot feel nearly as sure. As we have seen, he was second to no one in his appreciation of native folk-music and in conscientious desire to turn it to account in art-music. Though he went further than any other composer in the embodiment of actual folk-songs in his compositions, he was no more satisfied with this than Mussorgsky was. Even more literally than Glinka, he wished to "write music in Russian"—and we must concede at once that he did naturally absorb a great deal of the idiom. No musician, preoccupied with popular music as he was, could have failed to do so. But as one so often notices in Rimsky-Korsakov's work, the coldly intellectual element intervenes; beside this natural absorption there is a large proportion of artificial imitation. In other words, it is clear that Rimsky-Korsakov was sometimes guilty of the cold-blooded concoction of synthetic pseudo-folk-songs. There can be no doubt on this point;

he admits it in his memoirs, amusingly enough, in defending himself against the charge of having used too many actual folk-melodies in his early operas, an accusation brought forward by contemporary critics as evidence of the poverty of his melodic invention. It is curious that he failed to see how his defence went to prove that there was more than a grain of truth in the hostile criticisms. "As regards the invention of folk-songish melodies," he says, "they must naturally be based on the curves and motives of genuine folk-songs." And he goes on to ask naïvely, if with irrefragable logic, "how two things can resemble each other as wholes, if they do not resemble each other in any single detail? Hence: how can any melody be 'folk-songish' if its separate curves are not copied from those of genuine folk-songs?" The real point at issue seems to have escaped him as completely as it escaped his critics.

If, however, a defender of Rimsky-Korsakov should come forward and say, "Here are two folk-songish melodies, not genuine folk-songs. One is the spontaneous invention of a composer soaked in the folk-idiom, the other has been artificially imitated by an expert who also happens to be an artist.

Be good enough to tell me which is which," he might put the critic in a quandary. Superficially the natural tune might seem inferior to the artificial one; and in all probability it would be the less like a genuine folk-melody. The more fertile the composer, the less likely he would be to reproduce without adding something of his own. That is one of the tests by which we can sometimes detect the conscious imitator; he keeps too closely to his original. It never really becomes a living part of his own musical mind; it decorates his musical thought externally (and the decoration is "fixed," unchanging), but is not a part of its living, changing tissue. And so the artificiality betrays itself in his work as a whole, though melody for melody he may be able to turn out something which even the expert cannot distinguish from the genuine article. Apart altogether from Rimsky-Korsakov's implied admission, it is obvious that his creative faculty was never impregnated with the folk-idiom as thoroughly as Mussorgsky's was or he would never have been able to purge it away as he did in works like "Pan Voevoda" and "Servilia," to say nothing of dozens of pages of some of his most characteristic scores.

But the curious problems presented by the working of Rimsky-Korsakov's peculiar creative intelligence must be considered later in other aspects. For the present we must be content to sum up the results of his contact with folk-music as mainly superficial. In the best pages of his work—above all in "Sadko" and "Kitezh"—its influence has gone deeper, really saturating his thought. And before we dismiss the rest as "merely" decorative, it is only fair to remember its charm as decoration. One need not enjoy "Snegurochka" a jot the less because some of it is rather of the nature of musical patchwork. If Rimsky-Korsakov is here so much the less a creator, he is a particularly delightful compiler and arranger. There is no feeling of patchwork about the style of the work as a whole. No composer has ever known better than he how to make the most of given material of this nature. I emphasise the artificiality of his folk-song reproductions only because of the light it throws on his musical mind and in order to measure him in relation to an absolute standard of musical values.

And we may sum up the value of the folk-song element in classical Russian music as a whole in much the same way. The actual substance of folk-song embedded in it in one way or another is very considerable in bulk. Directly and indirectly, popular music has salted it through and through with simple, homely beauty, though not with that remote, mysterious beauty-with-authority which sets whatever possesses it on a plane apart. It is easy for the unfriendly critic to say that the path of folk-song led these composers nowhere. But they were not travelling to arrive—except at home like the man in Chesterton's story. They had something fresh to say and folk-song gave them the words to say it in. To one—Mussorgsky—it gave almost all the language he needed, and in varying degrees it enriched the vocabularies of all the others.

IV.—"THE STONE GUEST."

DARGOMÏZHSKY'S "Kamenniy Gost" ("The Stone Guest") has a curious place in the history of Russian music. It is one of those works which are landmarks without being masterpieces. One cannot read half-a-dozen pages about classical Russian opera without coming across some reference to it. Yet hardly anyone outside Russia knows it, and even in Russia itself it has never been more than a museum piece. It is true that it is constituted the operatic "Gospel" of the "mighty handful" and that, according to Cui, it was "the keystone of the new Russian operatic school." But even the Kuchkisti did not carry their admiration to the point of imitation. Mussorgsky, of all the younger men the most in sympathy with Dargomïzhsky's longing for "the expression of truth. . . truth and realism . . . the note as the direct equivalent of the word," attempted only one music drama on the lines of "The Stone Guest," his setting of

Gogol's "Marriage." And he lost interest in that after a month's work on it.* In Mussorgsky's later operas the element of Dargomïzhskian "truth" is mingled with others, lyrical and epic, and it is significant that there is less of it in "Khovanshchina" than in "Boris," while the fragmentary "Fair of Sorochintsi" was apparently to have been almost wholly lyrical. Rimsky-Korsakov flirted with Dargomïzhsky's style and methods throughout his career, as he did with Glinka's and, later, with Wagner's. Borodin did not even pay lip-service to Dargomïzhsky's principles. In short, this "recitative in three acts," as Lenz called "The Stone Guest," served the younger men less as a model than as a standard of reference. There it stood, a fixed point by which they could steer; but none of them cared to make straight for it. But since it has this historical importance and a sort of reputation at second-hand, it is worth at least cursory study.

"The Stone Guest" was the third and last opera of a composer even more the dilettante than his friend, Glinka. His first opera, "Esmeralda"

---

* It is only fair to admit that such an authority as Calvocoressi attributes the abandonment of "Marriage" to Mussorgsky's growing interest in "Boris."

(finished in 1839, but not produced till 1847) was, on his own confession, "weak and often trivial, in the style of Halévy and Meyerbeer," though he felt that "the most dramatic scenes already show some traces of that realistic style I have since tried to develop in my Russian music." His next, if we neglect an opera-ballet *manqué*, "The Triumph of Bacchus," was "The Russalka" (1856), which still keeps a place in the Russian repertoire, thanks to the vehicle it offers to Chaliapin's art in the rôle of the miller. In "The Russalka" Dargomïzhsky's lyric gifts are seen to be so conspicuously weak that a hostile critic might suggest that, in turning his back on pure melody in "The Stone Guest," he was merely making a virtue of necessity. But that would be definitely unfair. Dargomïzhsky's leaning toward the dramatic was natural, not the result of his lyrical weakness—except in so far as every artist is compelled by his weaknesses to concentrate on his strengths. Some of his songs of the late 'forties and early 'fifties show strongly dramatic tendencies. And even while he was writing "The Russalka," very much under Glinka's influence, he protested to a correspondent that Glinka understood only the lyrical element of Russian folk-music and had neglected its humorous and dramatic sides.

But Dargomïzhsky suffered from his environment. However individual an artist may be, he needs understanding friends as a plant needs soil. Even a Wagner needs encouragement, and Dargomïzhsky was no Wagner. Except Glinka, Dargomïzhsky for the greater part of his life mixed only with his artistic inferiors. His admirers were amateurs who must have praised his music for its weaknesses and who could hardly have been capable of sympathy with the progressive tendencies which have won Dargomïzhsky his place in the history books. It was not till the beginning of 1868, at the age of fifty-five, that he found the right sympathetic environment among his juniors, Balakirev, Stassov and their circle. And then it was too late; he was to be granted only another year of life—and that clouded by ill-health.

There is a certain pathos about Dargomïzhsky's gathering the younger men about him and writing his swan-song before their eyes. They met regularly at his house and Rimsky-Korsakov has told how "The Stone Guest" grew from week to week and how it was tried out, the composer singing Don Juan in his "hoarse tenor,"* Mussorgsky taking Leporello and Don Carlos, General Velyaminov (a keen amateur) the Monk and the Commander, and Alexandra Purgold, Laura and Donna Anna—with Nadezhda Purgold (afterwards Mme. Rimsky-Korsakov) at the piano. One fact is curious: Dargomïzhsky had thought of setting Pushkin's "little tragedy" as early as 1863 but, dilettante that he was, had been frightened by the magnitude of the task, though he was in perfectly good health. Now, early in 1868, a sick man, he composed three-quarters of the opera in two and a half months. He wrote to the singer, Karmalina, that his nervous condition seemed to generate one idea after another. "I have scarcely any physical strength left. . . . It is not I who write but some unknown force of which I am the instrument." A curious statement from a composer, never very spontaneous, about a work which has every appearance of having been calculated rather than created. However, the "unknown force" failed him in the autumn and, during the last few months of his life, Dargomïzhsky never

* Glinka speaks of Dargomizhsky, when he first met him in 1834, as "a little man with a sharp, piercing voice."

had sufficient strength to finish the first scene of Act I. It remained for Cui to add the last sixty bars or so, and for Rimsky-Korsakov, in scoring the work, to fill out some passages which the composer had merely sketched.*

The plan of Pushkin's "little tragedy" or "essay in dramatic investigation," "The Stone Guest," is very simple. The first scene of the first act is played before a monastery in Madrid. Don Juan, banished for the murder of the Commander (who in Pushkin's version is the husband, not the father, of Donna Anna), has returned to Madrid in disguise. He is speaking to Leporello of a dead love, Inez, when a monk appears and asks them if they are waiting for Donna Anna, who comes every day to pray for her dead husband's soul. She appears momentarily and piques Juan's curiosity. In the second scene we meet another lady, the actress Laura, whose part in the drama seems to be quite inessential; she is introduced, apparently, only to sing a couple of Spanish songs and to give Don Juan a further opportunity of demonstrating his power over

* "The Stone Guest" had its first performance at the Maryinsky Theatre, Petersburg, on February 16, (O.S.), 1872. Theodore Komissarzhevsky the elder, father of the famous producer and of Vera Komissarzhevsky, was the Don Juan.

the other sex. Laura, a former love of Juan's, is entertaining guests, one of whom, Don Carlos, she keeps back when the others go. But Don Carlos's pleasant evening is interrupted by the appearance of Don Juan. He and Carlos fight, the latter is killed, and the fickle Laura easily consoles herself once more with Juan. In the second act we see Don Juan, disguised as a monk, waiting by the Commander's statue for Donna Anna. When she comes he first addresses her respectfully in character with his dress, then makes love to her as "Don Diego." Finally she gives him an appointment for the following day, and when she has gone he mockingly invites the statue to come too, to stand sentinel at his widow's door. The third act consists of the scene in Anna's room, with the coming of the statue to exact vengeance.

Dargomïzhsky's way of going to work was really breath-taking in its daring simplicity. He simply set Pushkin's text, just as it stands, to what he accurately claimed to be "melodic recitative," declamation to definite musical rhythms and preserving some sense of melodic contour. As Calvocoressi has pointed out, the only parallel to such an undertaking (except Rimsky-Korsakov's "Mozart and

Salieri" and Mussorgsky's fragment of "Marriage") is Debussy's "Pelleas and Melisande" of more than thirty years later. But "melodic recitative," to be of any value, must be written by a man whose faculty of musical creation works in a peculiar way, to whom words naturally suggest music (living music, not a mere formula for declamation), yet with whom the music never takes the bit in its mouth, so to speak, and runs away with things. Mussorgsky, Borodin, Rimsky-Korsakov could all do this intermittently, but probably no composer has yet lived who could do it continuously. Dargomïzhsky certainly does not convince one that he had a peculiar genius for this species of composition. Try as he will to avoid the stereotyped, he cannot keep his recitative genuinely melodic. There are frequent lapses into dry declamation and too few compensating slips into genuine living melody. Except Laura's two songs (the first, by the way, preluded by a snatch of that *jota aragonesa* on which Glinka based his orchestral "Capriccio"), the vocal line is infused with genuine musical life and warmth only for a few bars here and there, as in Juan's love-making to Anna or in some of the monk's phrases. The monk's music has a character of its own, broad and unfolding for the most part in notes of even value. But, generally speaking, Dargomïzhsky failed to achieve *characterisation* in recitative as Mussorgsky, and even Rimsky-Korsakov frequently did. Dargomïzhsky's note for word translation of Pushkin into music is "true" in declamation, never emotionally false and sometimes very graphic—as in Leporello's gasping invitation to the statue. But though the notes may be the "direct expression of the speech," they only occasionally express the nature of the person who utters it. The feeling expressed by the vocal line is not only weak but generally impersonal, a curious result of such longing for *drama.*

Nor does the orchestra help the voices much. There is no question of the orchestra's expressing, or attempting to express, "that emotion which the spoken word cannot express,"* as with Wagner. The orchestra supplies an unobtrusive accompaniment, occasionally a commentary, hardly anything more. There is no prelude, though Rimsky-Korsakov thought it necessary to write one, based on material from the opera, for his

---

* Wagner: "Opera and Drama."

second edition of the score. Eight bars of introduction, which may mean anything or nothing, and Don Juan is speaking. And it is typical of Dargomïzhsky's score that these few bars of "marking time," a mere musical commonplace, recur here and there throughout the first scene, not to make a dramatic point, but simply as padding cut from the same piece of musical material. A hardly more significant figure seems to be always associated with Don Juan's memories of his "poor Inez":

Ex. 13.

And yet both these apparently platitudinous fragments are worth noting, since they show Dargomïzhsky's fondness for the sharpened fifth of the scale, for the augmented triad which is, so to speak, the "common chord" of the whole-tone scale which plays such an important part later in the work. Dargomïzhsky toys with the leit-motif: a little figure of four chords associated with Donna Anna:

Ex. 14.

another chord-progression associated first with the true monk, later with Don Juan in his monkish disguise; and so on. But his motives are mere inexpressive tags. They have no character. They do not cling about one's memory, calling up the past to enrich the present whenever we hear them. Dargomïzhsky sees *how* to make some extremely effective point but he is not good enough a musician actually to bring it off. There is an instance at the end of the first act. Juan and Laura embrace and go into another room, but the orchestra adds a significant last word before the curtain falls slowly on the empty stage. Now this stormy, passionate epilogue is based on the phrases to which Carlos has sung the words, "I, Don Carlos," and in which he has reminded Laura that she will enjoy only a few more years of youth, and the music to which he died in the duel; the idea was a stroke of dramatic genius. Yet it fails because of the sheer inadequacy of the music. In fact, Dargomïzhsky fails here in a dramatic moment for precisely the same reason that he fails earlier in the same scene to catch the glamour of the moonlit night in the love scene between Carlos and Laura; the music is dry and almost lifeless. But there are some striking dramatic details in "The Stone Guest": the very "modern" chromatic side-slipping of diminished sevenths at Anna's anxious "Diego, what is it?" as Juan gradually admits his identity in the last act, and an incessant chromatic quintuplet figure which admirably expresses their emotional agitation.

The most striking fruit of Dargomïzhsky's intellectualism is, of course, his devising of themes in the whole-tone scale, apparently symbolising the stoniness of the statue. As we have seen, Glinka had used the scale *as a scale* in "Ruslan," and the younger men were, for the most part, content to do no more. Rimsky-Korsakov introduces a descending whole-tone scale for expressive purposes in "May Night" and, with diatonic trimmings, in "Scheherazade" (the opening theme associated with the harsh Sultan Schariar). Borodin does the same in the accompaniment to his song, "Falshivaya Nota." Dargomïzhsky must be given whatever credit attaches to the distinction of having been the first to use, not the scale itself, but whole-tone themes. And even he, a man bold enough to write a whole opera without a single key-signature,* tackled the harmonic implications of the system very half-heartedly. We first hear the "statue" theme in Act II, between Leporello's anxious: "But the Commander? . . . . What will he say about it?":

Ex. 15.

Later, at the point where the statue nods acceptance, Dargomïzhsky does actually manage to write entirely in the whole-tone mode (see Ex. 16). The appearance of the statue in the last act is accompanied by a whole-tone chord (A flat, B flat, D, F sharp) held for two bars *fortissimo*, and as it

* Dargomïzhsky might almost be hailed as the pioneer of atonalism. But he would have saved himself trouble on a good many pages of "The Stone Guest" if he had followed the normal practice as regards notation.

DARGOMÏZHSKY

steps into the room there is a terrific outburst with a triplet bass moving in whole-tones. All this was

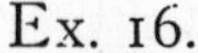
Ex. 16.

very bold for the 'sixties; Dargomïzhsky went a long way farther than Glinka had done. But, like him, he only used the whole-tone scale in passing, for a definite and limited expressive purpose. He could never have imagined, as Debussy seems to have done, that it might be employed as a self-sufficient, though limited, musical vocabulary in itself.

Apart altogether from the intrinsic value of "The Stone Guest" itself, apart from Dargomïzhsky's sheer musical incapacity to realise his own ideals, one cannot help doubting the value of a theory which leads to such a result when carried to its logical conclusion. Even when practised by a musician of far greater power, as in "Boris," this kind of realism cannot be kept up for long. Mere "literal translation" of words into music is not enough. It is no more likely to produce music worth calling such than literal translation of poetry into another language is likely to produce poetry. And verse wedded to music of this kind is, on the whole, less effective than spoken verse. It loses more than it gains. Tchaïkovsky was not so very far wrong when he spoke of the "unsuccessful attempt to drag *truth* into this sphere of art, in which everything is based upon falsehood, and 'truth,' in the everyday sense of the word, is not required at all." A play of any kind demands our acceptance of conventions. Poetic drama asks us to accept a great deal, and even the most realistic forms of music-drama still more than that. And since we must accept a convention of some kind, it surely does not matter very much what the convention is. All we ask is that the composer shall make the best of it. And if the history of opera teaches him anything at all, it is that the only way to succeed is, not by striving for "truth," but by exerting his musical power so as to make us forget the "lie." The striving for an illusory "truth" which is a recurrent feature of the history of opera (Rameau, Gluck, Wagner, Dargomïzhsky and Mussorgsky) is more valuable as a corrective to extreme artificiality than for its own sake.

It is, of course, impossible to discuss Dargomïzhsky's theories without thinking of Wagner's. The obvious idea that must occur to everyone—it occurred to Serov and other hostile critics in Dargomïzhsky's own lifetime—is that Dargomïzhsky was merely a disingenuous disciple of Wagner. And it must be admitted that there is evidence for, as well as against, that view of him. His use of the leit-motif cannot be allowed to count for much; he is just as likely to have taken the hint from Glinka. But it is absurd to point out, as some of Dargomïzhsky's apologists have done, that as Wagner's music was very little known in Russia at this time Dargomïzhsky must have been almost wholly ignorant of it. In any case it is Wagner's theories, rather than his scores, which are in question. But in 1864-5 Dargomïzhsky was in Western Europe—Leipzig, Paris, Brussels, London—and must have had ample opportunities of discussing Wagner, if not of seeing his operas. Wagner was then the most talked of musician in Europe. Is it likely that anyone so deeply interested in operatic problems as Dargomïzhsky was, neglected any chance of finding out all he could about him? After all, the piano score of "Das Rheingold" had been available since 1861. And we know that Dargomïzhsky was acquainted with "Tannhäuser" as early as 1856, for in that year we find him writing to Serov, "I have not returned your score of 'Tannhäuser,' as I have not yet had time to look through the whole of it. You are right; there is a great deal of poetry in the scenario and also in the music. But the spicy melodies are unnatural, and although the harmonies are sometimes very interesting, one is conscious of the effort—*will und kann nicht!* Truth—truth before all—but we have a right to expect good taste as well,"—a criticism which might be applied even more fittingly to his own "Stone Guest"!

We have Rimsky-Korsakov's word for it that when Dargomïzhsky attended the first Petersburg performance of "Lohengrin," only two or three months before his death, he "poured out on it his inexhaustible store of humour, mockery and venomous comment." There is no reason to accuse Dargomïzhsky of jealousy or moral dishonesty on that account, however, though the story does leave a nasty taste in the mouth. He may have genuinely disliked Wagner's music, and he must have delighted in the consciousness that his own "Stone Guest" was far more "advanced" and unconventional than this very lyrical work of Wagner's. But, however many hints he may have taken from Wagner's theories, Dargomïzhsky's operatic style has hardly more in common with Wagner's than the Russian language with the German. His subordination of the orchestra to the voice is alone sufficient to mark a vital difference caused by something more than the musical inequality of the two composers. Musically, of course, Dargomïzhsky owed nothing, or next to nothing, to Wagner. In the whole of "The Stone Guest" there are only two passages that even remotely suggest Wagnerian influence: Don Juan's cry, "Alas! A victim of hopeless passion," in Act III (Ex. 17), and the orchestral passage, pallidly Wagnerian in both its sequential treatment and its rising chromatic excitement, when, thinking of the dead Inez, Juan recalls "the curious charm of her pale lips and serious eyes."

Ex. 17.

V.—TOLSTOY AND MUSSORGSKY.

EVER since Plutarch men have amused themselves by drawing parallels between the great. It is at bottom merely a pastime, an intellectual game which at the same time allows scope —too much—for the play of the imagination. But it is not quite an empty sport; like other games it is a discipline and an education. To change the metaphor: if our travelling leads us nowhere, we at least see many things on the way. But one danger above all is to be guarded against. "It is," says Bacon, "the vice of high and discursive intellects"—and others, maybe—"to attach too much importance to slight resemblances; when this is indulged to excess it leads men to catch at shadows instead of substances." Moreover, in comparing two such men as Tolstoy and Mussorgsky, who were not only compatriots but contemporaries,* there is always the

* Tolstoy was about ten years older than Mussorgsky, though he survived him by nearly thirty years.

risk of attributing to individuals ideas and beliefs generally current and belonging to the common stock.* Here, common sense and one's more or less defective knowledge of the period are one's only safeguards.

The coincidence of Mussorgsky's conception of art and his methods of artistic procedure with Tolstoy's may be partially due to the circumstances in which both lived, but even if it were wholly so, the identity of ideas between Russia's greatest novelist and her greatest dramatic musician would be hardly less interesting. The agreement is not limited to one or two striking points; it is extraordinarily complete. Insistence on the unimportance of beauty in art; the conception of the function of art as "a means of conversing with one's fellow-men"; contempt for technique, even as a means; a strong leaning toward realism; a tendency to make the masses more important than individual characters or to value individuals in proportion as they are representative of the masses; over-valuation of the peasant-type—all these are equally characteristic of

* No doubt both were influenced by the theories of the critics Chernyshevsky (1828-1889) and Dobrolyubov (1836-1861), champions of artistic realism.

Tolstoy and Mussorgsky. It is true that all these heterogeneous theories, instincts and prejudices are (or, at least, can be shown to be) more or less logically connected. But, man being the illogical animal he is, that hardly makes the coincidence less striking.

Let us take these points one by one; first the contempt for beauty as the end and aim of the serious artist. When the seventy-year-old Tolstoy wrote "What is Art?" he took this as his starting-point. His method was simple enough. He catalogued all the known definitions of beauty, from Baumgarten's to those of contemporary æstheticians, and pointed out that they might be boiled down to two fundamental conceptions, "the one objective, mystical, that beauty is one of the manifestations of the absolutely Perfect, of the Idea, of the Spirit, of Will, or of God—a fantastic definition, founded on nothing; the other, on the contrary, a very simple, and intelligible, subjective one, which considers beauty to be that which pleases." And he concluded that "to see the aim and purpose of art in the pleasure we get from it, is like assuming that the purpose and aim of food is the pleasure derived when consuming it." Mussorgsky had, by whatever chain of reasoning (or none), come to the same conclusion a quarter of a century earlier, for we find him writing to Stassov in 1872 that "the artistic representation of mere beauty, in the material sense of the word, is sheer childishness, a rudimentary form of art." His conception of the artist's business, outlined in this letter and later ones to the same correspondent, is not that of the Tolstoy of "What is Art?" but it exactly describes the attitude of the earlier Tolstoy of the great novels: "Life, wherever it manifests itself; truth, however unpleasant; daring, plain-speaking before everyone *à bout portant*—that is what I aim at." Again: "The masses, like individuals, present subtle traits, difficult to fathom, not yet grasped. To distinguish them, to learn to read them at sight, by observation and hypothesis, to study their inmost recesses, to feed mankind with them as with an as-yet-unknown health-giving food—that is the task, the supreme joy!" And in his brief autobiography Mussorgsky states his "profession of artistic faith" as the belief that "art is a means of conversing with men, and not an end in itself," which exactly anticipates Tolstoy's conclusion in "What is Art?"

Now this view of art is essentially that of philosophical optimism—probably unconscious in Mussorgsky's case, all too self-conscious in Tolstoy's. Life is real; life is earnest; and everything which in no way helps humanity toward its goal is mere child's play. Carlyle said something to the same effect about the Waverley novels. It was the old Puritan view. And the pessimistic view harmonises curiously with it. In the very year that Mussorgsky finished "Boris," the young Nietzsche—not yet out of his Schopenhauerian-Wagnerian leading-strings—had written his first book, "The Birth of Tragedy," to prove that great art (that is, *beautiful* art) springs only from the soil of pessimism. Confronted with a real world of imperfection, contradiction and ultimate chaos, man is compelled to make something whole and perfect and harmonious *for himself*.* Nietzsche traces the decline of Greek art from the appearance of Socrates, the "theoretical optimist." Once the universe could be shown to admit of a logical explanation, art was no longer regarded as a necessity but as mere child's play.

In various notes and sketches dating from the

* "My melancholy seeks repose in the hiding-places and abysses of *perfection*; for that purpose I need music," he wrote years afterwards.

same period.* Nietzsche makes his position still clearer. He, too, concludes that beauty exists only in our own "consciousness of pleasure." But, far from beauty being truth, truth beauty, the sole function of the beautiful (hence, the sole object of art) is to cover reality, the terrible truth, with a veil of illusion.† "The further a thing is from real existence, the more pure, beautiful and good it is. . . . It is not possible to live with truth; the Will to Truth is a symptom of degeneracy." Incidentally, Nietzsche attributes classic art to the "pessimism of strength," the artist rejoicing in the knowledge that he alone can create perfection, and traces romantic art from the "pessimism of weakness," the artist brooding sentimentally over an imperfect world. So, if we like, we can reconcile Nietzsche with Tolstoy to our own satisfaction by assuming that great

* Published in Vols. IX and XIV of the German edition of his complete works.

† Compare with this one of Rimsky-Korsakov's most self-revealing remarks, reported by Yastrebtsev: "You would scarcely find anyone in the world who believes less in everything supernatural, fantastic or lying beyond the boundaries of death than I do—yet as an artist I love this sort of thing above all else. And religious ceremonial—what could be more intolerable? . . . . And yet with what love I have expressed such ceremonial customs in music! No, I am actually of the opinion that art is essentially the most enchanting, intoxicating lie." Nothing could show more clearly the difference between Rimsky-Korsakov's outlook and Mussorgsky's.

art may be either classic, romantic, or optimistic in origin.

So much for theorising. But the important point is that contempt for beauty as the end of art, and striving after "truth" or "realism," are shown to be logical consequences of an optimistic *Weltanschauung*. We have seen that Mussorgsky, like Zola, wanted to take for his subjects "life, wherever it manifests itself, and truth, however unpleasant," and we know that Tolstoy did so, achieving his effects by minute observation and analysis and the accumulation of an infinite number of accurately rendered details. But the musical realist cannot go about things in quite the same way. There *is* a kind of musical realism, which Mussorgsky exploited to the full in several of the "Exhibition Pictures" for piano, in some of his songs, and in a few passages of "Boris Godunov" and "Khovanshchina," but depending as it does so largely on arbitrary association of musical with non-musical ideas, we can only smile at it as we do at Haydn's "sinuous worm" and Strauss's windmill. Mussorgsky's genuine realism is revealed in his choice of subjects and in his handling of his artistic materials. As he claimed, he took all life for his province, not merely those facets of it which tradition and convention have marked out as peculiarly suitable for artistic treatment. He wrote songs about children, about death-chambers, about the sorrows of village idiots, and about musical critics. And if, like the French literary "realists" and "naturalists," his choice of subjects betrays a leaning to the morbid and sordid, he never made the mistake, as they did, of supposing that anything is interesting simply because it is "life." Nor did Tolstoy. Both had the true artist's ability to select carefully while appearing to pick at random. "Realism" and "truth" are not necessarily synonyms for the same quality in art. For that matter, realism is not an affair of quality at all, but of quantity. All art is a compromise between phenomena presented to the senses or to the mind: shapes, colours, emotions, musical ideas or what not, and certain arbitrary limits and conventions: five acts, sonata form, a rectangular canvas, metre, a certain number of instruments. It is for each artist to decide how near or how far from nature he is to fix his compromise—the nearer, the more realistic his work will be; and artistic truth consists in being true, not to nature (which is impossible), but to whatever compromise has been adopted. Mussorgsky, in his unvarying practice, and Tolstoy, theorising at the end of his creative career, gave their votes unhesitatingly in favour of the minimum of stylisation. The less technique was brought into play in converting the raw material of nature into the finished work of art the better.

Naturally, therefore, both detested the worship of technique for its own sake. Mussorgsky thought musicians were worse than other artists in this respect. "Tell me," he asks Stassov, "why, when I listen to the conversation of young artists, painters, or sculptors, I can follow their thoughts and understand their opinions and aims, and I seldom hear them mention technique, save in certain cases of absolute necessity? On the other hand, when I find myself among musicians I rarely hear them utter a living idea; one would think they were still at school; they know nothing of anything but technique and 'shop-talk.' Is the art of music so young that it has to be studied in this puerile way?" Tolstoy, in his downright, bludgeoning style, says: "A man in our time, if only he possesses a certain amount of ability and selects some speciality, may, after learning the methods of counterfeiting used in his branch of art, turn out unceasingly to the end of his life works which will pass for art in our society. To produce such counterfeits, definite rules or recipes exist in each branch of art. So the talented man, having assimilated them, may produce such works *à froid*, cold-drawn, without feeling."* When in a later chapter of "What is Art?" he looked to "the artist of the future, who will be free from all the perversion of technical improvements concealing the absence of subject-matter, and who, not being a professional artist, will only produce art when he feels impelled to do so by an irresistible inner impulse," he did not realise that such an artist had died in Russia seventeen years before. It would be difficult to imagine music more free from ready-made (or even self-made) formulas of expression than Mussorgsky's is. As Debussy put it, his music "ressemble à un art de curieux sauvage qui découvrirait la musique à chaque pas tracé par son émotion." Whether Tolstoy was acquainted with Mussorgsky's work I do not know; possibly he knew it without recognising it as what he wanted.

* In these quotations from Tolstoy's "What is Art?" I have availed myself of Mr. Aylmer Maude's translation (World's Classics): the translations from Mussorgsky's letters are my own.

At any rate he dismissed Pushkin's "Boris," on which Mussorgsky based his opera, as "a cold, brain-spun work."

Both Tolstoy and Mussorgsky were obviously realists by artistic instinct. But both were also conscious that stylisation and technical ingenuity, necessary in art devoted to the ideal of beauty, were only an encumbrance to art intended as a "means of conversing with one's fellow-men." They were consciously at war with everything which limits the appeal of art. Art which appealed only to the cultured few seemed to them artificial and even ridiculous. They detested preciousness. Tolstoy devoted heated pages to the destruction of Baudelaire, Verlaine and Mallarmé (such a bull in such a china-shop!); and we find Mussorgsky exercising his sarcasm at the expense of artists "the whole of whose aspirations is comprised in the distilling, one by one, of even little drops" and who "take no interest in the essentials of life."* "People more useless to contemporary art are not to be found, I should think, even in the celestial realm."

* This blow seems to have been aimed principally at Rimsky-Korsakov, with whom Mussorgsky was then (1875) completely out of sympathy, and at Tchaïkovsky.

Tolstoy was prepared to reduce to absurdity his theory that art should be universal in appeal, by setting up his favourite type, the "unperverted peasant," as a sounder judge of art than a cultured man "whose taste has been atrophied by his education and life." It is doubtful whether Mussorgsky would have preferred such critics even to those he ridiculed in "The Musician's Peep-Show" and "The Classicist," but he fully shared Tolstoy's admiration for the type. After his death his brother told Stassov, "In his years of childhood and youth as in middle age, my brother Modest always felt a particular sympathy with our peasants; he considered the Russian *muzhik* a *genuine human being*." Perhaps he was over-conscious of the peasant-blood, from his paternal grandmother, in his own veins.

Mussorgsky's and Tolstoy's admiration of the people had yet another consequence. Tolstoy not only desired that art should be comprehensible to the masses; in his novels, above all in "War and Peace," he, so to speak, dramatised mass feeling. He had a theory of necessity and free-will which is summarised by Mr. Aylmer Maude in the introduction to his translation of "War and Peace": "Not only historic life, but all human life, is directed not only by intelligence or will—that is, not by thoughts or wishes that have reached a clearly conscious form —but by something mysterious and strong, the so-called nature of man. The sources of life, both of individuals and of whole peoples, are much profounder and more potent than the conscious choice and conscious reflection which apparently guides people." So, whereas the pessimist braces his will, shuts out compassion and rests all his hopes on the culture of the individual, the optimist comfortably sees salvation in sympathy with the instincts of the masses. The subject of "War and Peace" is the blindly achieved triumph of the Russian people, in spite of their leaders and even in spite of themselves. The real heroes of the book are those—from Kutuzov, the commander-in-chief, to the peasant-soldier, Karataev—who represent the mass-instinct of the Russian people.

Mussorgsky was expressing the same thought rather more vaguely (as becomes a musician) when he said that "the masses present subtle traits, difficult to fathom," and defined the artist's task as the study of these features and the "feeding of mankind" with them. We know how he carried out that task himself. It has become a commonplace of criticism to say that the real hero of "Boris Godunov" is the Russian people. But Mussorgsky had subordinated individuals to masses in earlier works than "Boris." Stassov tells us that in "Salammbô" (1863-4), of which Mussorgsky wrote only the "book" and a few numbers, "according to the libretto, all these scenes, filled with dramatic movement in Meyerbeer's style, depicted great masses of people at moments of emotional excitement; the scenes between the principal characters were of less importance." Although in the later "Khovanshchina" more importance is given to individuals, they are important as representatives rather than for their own sakes. The tragedy lies not so much in the fall of the Khovanskys and the destruction of the Old Believers as in the passing of the older Russia they stand for. Mussorgsky appears to have progressed from opera in which masses were employed for their own sake, because the handling of masses gave him pleasure as an artist, to opera in which the masses or their representatives were used as visible symbols of what he conceived to be the profoundest currents of national feeling.

But after all they are curious people, these artists who are so painfully conscious of what they are doing. They do it so well, so thoroughly—yet so unlike artists. They will have nothing of the labour of technique, yet they labour like ants at the accumulation of correct, matter-of-fact detail. It would be unjust to compare "War and Peace" with Frith's "Derby Day," but in this matter-of-factness lies the secret weakness of both Tolstoy and Mussorgsky as creative artists. It is far more serious in the man whose medium is music than in the man who works in prose. It is (if one may be forgiven such a glimpse of the obvious) in the nature of prose to be prosaic, but prosaic music—recitative, for instance, or "The Market Place at Limoges"—is only half music. No one realised that more clearly than Tolstoy, and one is left with an amused feeling that he might have approved of the more lyrical (that is, the more beautiful) pages of "Boris" and "Khovanshchina" as "simple, clear and powerful music," but would have condemned the inn-scene in "Boris," the baiting of the Simpleton, and songs like "Savishna" and "The Orphan," in which beauty is subordinated to truth, in much the same terms as those he applied to Wagner's "Forest Murmurs"—"absolutely unintelligible musically."

VI.—BORODIN AS A SYMPHONIST.

WHEN Tolstoy asked and answered the question, "What is Art?" he proved nothing but the impossibility of defining the infinite. We define art and the things that belong to it in terms of ourselves; my definition is little more than a statement of my own limitations. "What is a symphony?" There is no definition (because there is an infinite number of definitions). It may be almost anything, from what the dictionary says to Mahler's "Mir heisst Symphonie mit allen Mitteln der vorhandenen Technik mir eine Welt aufbauen."* We can only fall back on common sense and say we can recognise a symphony when we hear one.

Most people—unless they take the rather severe view of the gentleman who held that Franck's D minor could not really be a symphony because the score included a *cor anglais*—will agree that

* "For me a 'symphony' means the building up of a world, using every available means."

Borodin's three works are genuine symphonies. Yet Dvorák, who was not narrowly academic, once remarked to James Huneker that Tchaïkovsky was really a composer of suites—and we understand perfectly well what he meant. Instead of asking, "What is a symphony?" we must ask what is essential to a *good* symphony. What differentiates it beyond dispute from a suite, for instance? Now the answer seems fairly obvious. The material must be worthy of a large fabric (as the second subject of Tchaïkovsky's "Pathétique" first movement is not); the construction must be closely knit, convincing in both its musical logic and its emotional sequence; the arrangement of both material and tonality must be balanced without being mechanical; above all, perhaps, the whole work must be greater than the sum of its separate movements. Perfectly true; yet let us "clear our minds of cant." We say the material must be genuinely symphonic; a man does not make a fresco painting of his pet canary. But how are we to judge it, musical themes being so much less concrete than canaries? A theme in Mozart's "Bastien et Bastienne" is obviously too trivial for symphonic use, while the same theme (apparently) in the "Eroïca" is tremendous. Someone may say the difference lies in the subsequent treatment, but if so I shall beg to disagree. A succession of rhythmically arranged notes on paper is not in itself a composer's material. He thinks of the notes and feels them in a particular way (as regards texture as well as *tempo* and inflexion). Beethoven's way of feeling those four bars was entirely different from Mozart's, therefore his theme is not the same. Here is a theme, typical of many of Borodin's ideas, from the finale of his Second Symphony :—

Ex. 18.

It is first stated by a solo clarinet and appears on paper to be an ordinary "cantabile contrast" second subject. You can think of it as that—and if you do its subsequent treatment will no doubt fill you with quite justifiable horror, while a performance under a conductor who took the same view (and he might point to the last *dolce* appearance of the tune in self-defence) would never suggest to you that you were wrong. Only if you feel that theme as the fragment of naked savagery it is, do you recognise the perfect fitness, the inevitability, of Borodin's treatment of it.

That is one form of "cant," the judgment of sound by the appearance on paper of symbols which may mean one thing or some other quite different. There are others—one of them is the superstition, not yet dead, that formal symmetry is more or less a matter of counting bars—but they must pass. To free oneself entirely from cant is hardly possible, but a mind hampered by preconceived ideas on inessential points can scarcely appreciate justly the symphonic work of a composer like Borodin. Not that his symphonies are startlingly unconventional; if they were it would probably simplify matters. It is the apparent almost-usualness which makes the essential difference so liable to be misunderstood.

Let us for a moment recall a few dates and circumstances. Borodin, like Mussorgsky and Rimsky-Korsakov, was not a professional musician. The fact has less bearing on the technical quality of his work than unfriendly critics would have us believe (much that appears naïve and awkward in his work admits of other explanations),* but it does

* Tchaïkovsky's statement to Madame von Meck that "his technique is so poor that he cannot write a bar without assistance" can only be described as grotesque.

account for both the smallness of his output and the abnormal time spent over the larger works. The E flat Symphony took five years to complete, the B minor seven, a circumstance which explains the lack of unity of feeling in the earlier work and makes the splendid cohesion of the later one rather remarkable. When he began the E flat Symphony in 1862, at the age of twenty-eight, Borodin had only just met Balakirev. The Symphony was his first big composition and he embarked on it with no experience of orchestration. The Second, the well-known B minor (1869-1876), is roughly contemporaneous with "Prince Igor." The Third, in A minor, is a mere fragment, a *moderato assai* and scherzo completed and orchestrated by Glazunov. Both the E flat and B minor Symphonies were edited by Rimsky-Korsakov after the composer's death, and in view of what we know of his treatment of "Boris" one wonders how broad a view he took of an editor's function in this case also.* Whether

* The note on both scores, "Revue par N. Rimsky-Korsakov et A. Glazunov," may have quite a sinister significance. And Glinka's orchestral works are both *revues et corrigées*. Unless we are given the facts, all Russian music of the last century will in future rest under the suspicion of having been more or less written by Rimsky-Korsakov !

Borodin (or even Mussorgsky) would have been as annoyed with his friend as the theoretical purists are, is rather doubtful. We must not lose sight of the fact that interference with each other's work was a perfectly normal proceeding among the members of the "mighty handful," and it possibly never occurred to Rimsky-Korsakov that there was any essential difference between advising one's friends on the composition of their symphonies and operas while they were alive and revising their works when they were dead. To take only one instance: the opening of the scherzo of the B minor Symphony was devised by Balakirev, who felt that the key-contrast (B minor to F major) was too strong. And Borodin approved, although the reiterated C's on the horns, coming immediately after the terrific unison B natural with which the first movement closes, would be extremely effective. One can imagine what a howl would have gone up from the purists if the crime had been perpetrated after the composer's death. The fact that he did approve makes the interpolation none the less unfortunate, for it makes it more difficult to grasp the (apparently haphazard) tonal scheme of the whole symphony, based as it is on a sort of semitone *Rückung* of the type Schubert invented* and Bruckner worked to death. Borodin originally slipped directly from a long-held unison B natural to eight bars of unison C's, which was clear enough; then, the scherzo being in F, he opened the slow movement (D flat) with a G flat major chord. The movements are detached, but obviously the breaks should be made as short as possible. There is no break at all between slow movement and finale, the D flat-A flat of the final chord of the former being held (enharmonically, as C sharp-G sharp) through the first three bars of the latter—and we are home again in B major. Borodin had previously employed the same unusual juxtaposition of keys† in the E flat Symphony, where first movement and scherzo are in E flat but the slow movement is in D (its middle section sideslipping again to D flat), while the finale returns to the main key. In both works the scherzo precedes the slow movement, as it was evidently to do in the unfinished Third also. The key-scheme is here more

* See, for instance, his four-hand Fantasia in F minor, with its sideslip to F sharp minor.

† Rimsky-Korsakov's early symphonic poem, "Sadko," is planned with the key-scheme D flat-D-D flat. He tells us that he chose these particular keys because, with their relative minors, they were "Balakirev's favourite keys"—a fact which probably influenced Borodin as well.

conventional: first movement, A minor (but with the tonic major firmly established throughout the last 103 bars); scherzo, D major.

The invention and handling of the material and, in several cases, the organisation of the individual movements show the same vigour and individuality of thought. The First Symphony is not, it must be admitted, homogeneous; Dvorák might have complained with some justice that it is really a suite. The scherzo is second-hand Berlioz (though with a characteristic, folk-songish trio), the finale second-hand Schumann. The *andante* is picturesque and Oriental, genuine Borodin, but the rather saccharine, harmonically flabby Borodin who contrasts so extraordinarily with that other Borodin whose music sounds as if it might have been written by one of Gogol's Cossack heroes. But the first movement compensates—as far as one movement can compensate—for the weakness of the others.

First come twenty-eight bars of slow introduction, indefinite but portentous. Twice we hear a striking theme:—

Ex. 19.

on bassoons and lower strings. Everything else is vague and shifting—and then suddenly we break into the *allegro* in the major key. But what an *allegro!* Instead of an orthodox exposition we find we are already plunged into a premature development of Ex. 19—dissected and two of the pieces thrown at us simultaneously. Against an extraordinary chord rhythmically repeated for twelve bars (anticipating "The Planets" by over half a century):—

Ex. 20.

the drums play continually the second bar of Ex. 19, while the third bar is tossed to and fro between violins and violas. A *sforzando* chord—and the brass take up bar four:—

Ex. 21.

It is not till the twenty-eighth bar of the *allegro* that the theme is heard in a connected form, though even here only three bars of it appear. Flying fragments of the theme are driven contrapuntally against each other; bar four is worked as a bass, while bar three (with bar two for a few moments) is sent flying all over the orchestra. The tremendous rhythmic impetus carries the whole mass irresistibly forward.

And there we have one of the essential differences between Russian and German symphonic music. The forward impulse in a symphony by Beethoven or Brahms comes from the logic of the music—the linking up of long-breathed phrases, the unfolding of an idea, the gradual working toward a new key. If there is a dominating rhythm, as in the first movement of Beethoven's Seventh, its driving power is never depended on alone to carry the music along. With Borodin (and Stravinsky and all the most typically Russian composers) underlying rhythm is the only means used to give a sense of progress. All this ingenious analysis of his theme is a static business; when he goes into another key it is simply for the sake of variety—he modulates merely as he changes his orchestration; to use a bass as the fulcrum of a lever never occurs to him; when he writes (in Ex. 21) a progression which sounds as if it might really progress somewhere he uses it only to come back more emphatically to the chord he has just left and which he has been hammering home for the last dozen bars (Ex. 20).

Now this way of writing a symphonic movement admits of only two explanations; either the composer was hopelessly incompetent or he was looking at things from an angle altogether different from ours. To charge with incompetence a composer capable of the technical ingenuity displayed in this very movement is, of course, absurd—though it has taken half a century to convince the musical world that there was method in Mussorgsky's madness. Borodin was an amateur, but he was no mere dilettante like Glinka and Dargomïzhsky. Is it too much then to assume that his ideas on methods of symphonic construction were as original as, for example, his ideas concerning key-schemes and that he knew perfectly well what he was doing? (There *are* signs of immaturity in this *allegro*—weak chromatic meanderings and so on—but they are invariably trivial and incidental.) What then was he trying to do? Let us look first for a moment at the second subject. Here are the essential fragments:—

Ex. 22.

Their fairly obvious relationship is made clearer still when the second violins play (a) with the second bar in the rhythm of (b). Taken by themselves they are not big enough for a symphonic second subject; but we soon find that they are not to be taken by themselves. Before long the key-centre is shifted farther than it has been at all as yet; what sounds like an ordinary development begins and soon we get this sort of thing:—

Ex. 23.

(with horns and basses emphasising a pedal E

throughout) which shows that Ex. 22 (b) is simply a variation of the first bar of Ex. 19. The development is short, too short for the usual plan, but it is repeated (in a condensed form and chiefly in E flat) after the reprise. There is a big climax, the peak of the whole movement, with a new variation of the first two bars of Ex. 19 on the full orchestra :—

Ex. 24.

and then an *andantino* epilogue gives us the key to the whole puzzle :—

Ex. 25.

So it was all one then, after all! We have been shown the two main pieces separately; we have been teased with all sorts of hints that they were not such strangers as they seemed; we have been mocked with something that only *appeared* to be sonata form. Given the clue, everything is perfectly clear. Whereas the essence of first movement form as the great German masters understood it is duality, the drama arising from the juxtaposition of contrasted ideas, the essence of Borodin's first movements is unity. In this First Symphony he obtains it by that final synthesis after the elaborate analysis of his material; in the Second by allowing the extremely powerful opening theme (Ex. 1) to dominate the whole movement, so that the lyrical second subject:—

Ex. 26.

appearing but briefly, serves only to throw it into higher relief and in the development is itself immediately battered into the shape of the other:—

Ex. 27.

In addition, the B minor is more concise than the E flat and is stamped with a unity of mood which the other lacks. The *moderato* of the Third, the A minor, Symphony, is very square and conventional in outline, but Glazunov had to complete a rough sketch and did so as symmetrically as he could. Yet here again the unity of mood is striking; the secondary subjects, though unrelated to the chief theme, continue its mood, modifying rather than contrasting with it. Such variety as the movement has is obtained by changes of key or colour or dynamic force.

Such, then, are the ideas Borodin places on his canvases and his general conception of the symphonic first movement. Broadly speaking, he is content to use the conventional sonata form plan for the spacing out of his ideas, but in his hands, although (perhaps *because*) he uses it for a different end from that for which it was devised, it ceases to be a convention and becomes a living organism again. It is the general outline of sonata form, but nothing more. The real, as opposed to this apparent, shape of the movement emerges entirely from the material itself as it works to the foreseen goal—Ex. 25, with its gathering up of all the threads, in the First Symphony, the terrible, naked final statement of the principal theme in the Second, or the delicately coloured fading of day-dreams in the Third.

To compare a Borodin symphony with a Brahms, whether as a whole or in its parts, is like comparing St. Sophia at Kiev with Cologne Cathedral, or measuring "Anna Karenina" against "Madame Bovary." To prolong a dangerous parallel a little further, Borodin's musical organisms grow and live, and shape themselves in growing, not unlike novels. Yet no music is less literary in substance. Borodin may or may not have had in his mind a gathering of boyars, with their songs and feasting, in the B minor Symphony. He said so himself, but the explanation sounds like an afterthought. In any case, it is hopelessly inadequate. The finale is surely much more than a banquet of barbaric chieftains, gorgeously painted. (What the composer wrote here on lined paper counts for more than what he is reported to have said to Stassov.) Who could be so deaf as to hear their songs in that lovely, dreaming *andante*, which, if it is anything but pure music, is summer with its haze of heat, the drowsy summer of the Caucasus that Tolstoy paints in "The Cossacks"? We shall be on surer ground if we study the relationship to "Prince Igor," which was being written at the same period. The B minor Symphony sounds like a symphonic version of all that is best in "Prince Igor"—made a little better. How much finer is the *andante* of the Symphony, despite the harmonic weakness which it shares with most of Borodin's slow movements, than Vladimir's cavatina, for instance. As for the scherzo (parts of which would be perfectly in place if transferred to the Polovtsian dances), it is unique in orchestral literature. So, for that matter, is the entirely different one of the Third Symphony—a *moto perpetuo* in five-eight time (Ex. 2). To have created two such original scherzi, almost two new types of scherzo, would in itself have been a remarkable feat. But no composer less derivative than Borodin has ever lived.

VII.—"PRINCE IGOR."

BORODIN'S attention was first turned to the mediæval epic of Prince Igor, as a possible subject for an opera, by Stassov, who sent him a rough scenario in April, 1869. Acknowledging the receipt of this, the composer wrote to his friend that the subject "pleased him immensely." "Only will it be within my powers? I don't know. 'If you are afraid of wolves—don't go into the forest.' I will try." Accordingly he began the work in May of the same year. Yet at his death in 1887 the score was still unfinished—with some numbers in a fragmentary state, very little orchestrated, the overture not even put on paper (though it had been composed). It was the composer's third experiment in writing for the stage—the fourth if we reckon a parody-pastiche, "The Bohatyrs," largely based on music by Offenbach and others, which had one performance at the Grand Theatre in Moscow in 1867—for he had previously attempted a setting of Leo Mey's "The Tsar's Bride," on which Rimsky-Korsakov was afterwards to base one of his most popular works. And he had collaborated with Mussorgsky, Cui and Rimsky-Korsakov in the abortive "Mlada" of 1872, being responsible for the fourth act of that ill-fated venture.

From the beginning, Borodin realised that the subject of "Igor" was not altogether suitable for a dramatic purpose, but he loved it and, although he abandoned it more than once, always returned to his love. It can hardly be doubted that the B minor Symphony was the result of his despair of ever realising the "Igor" of his dreams. Perhaps in a sense the Symphony *was* the "Igor" of his dreams. Its first movement was written immediately after the first breakdown in the composition of the opera, and the Symphony in turn was interrupted by the commission to set Gedeonov's "Mlada" for the Imperial Theatre in Petersburg.* These three compositions are therefore closely related and there was even a certain amount of interchange of material between them. The "Mlada" music was based to a considerable extent on sketches originally made

* Gedeonov, the director of the theatre, was responsible only for the general scenario. The actual librettist was V. A. Krïlov —not to be confused with the author of the famous fables—who had also written the text of "The Bohatyrs."

for "Igor," and, when the "Mlada" project came to nothing, this material (together, apparently, with some of the new music written directly for "Mlada") was restored to the other opera.* Thus the opening of the Prologue is identical with the music associated with the priests in "Mlada"; the "eclipse" music was originally intended to accompany the appearance of the spirits of Prince Yaromir's ancestors; one of the themes in Yaroslavna's big *arioso* at the beginning of the second scene of Act I—it reappears in her duet with Igor in the last act—was the Yaromir motif itself; and part of the final chorus of "Igor" (that sung by the women's voices only) was written, or at any rate *used*, to accompany the procession of gods in "Mlada" in the final scene of the destruction of Radegast's temple by flood and tempest. Borodin even thought of using the "flood" music itself in the third act of "Igor." In the old chronicle, Igor converses with the river Don as he crosses it in his flight and Borodin had got hold of a tradition that the river overflowed its banks to check the pursuit of the Polovtsy.

* The other collaborators dealt with their contributions in the same free and easy way. And it is well known that a number of passages in "Boris Godunov" were originally composed for "Salammbô."

However, the composer wisely rejected the idea on further consideration and the music was orchestrated as a separate concert piece by Rimsky-Korsakov after Borodin's death. Incidentally, it was only after "Mlada" had fallen through that Borodin decided to provide "Igor" with a prologue. His original intention had been to write an epilogue, and the splendid "Slava" chorus at the beginning of the work was in the first place designed to end it.

"Slovo o Polku Igoreve"—the Song of the Army of Igor—is one of the oldest of Russian manuscript chronicles. When first printed, early in the nineteenth century,* its genuineness was doubted. It was greeted as the work of some Russian Ossian. But it is now universally accepted as a contemporary account, probably by a professional bard, of an actual historical event. As in the poems of Ossian, the story is told in rhythmic prose. Indeed an interesting parallel might be drawn between Macpherson's forgery (if it was a forgery) and this fragment from Russia's heroic age. "The poem abounds in great lyrical beauties," we are told, "as

* By the archæologist, Musin-Pushkin, who discovered the manuscript in the Spaso-Yaroslavsky Monastery in 1795. The manuscript itself was destroyed in the burning of Moscow in 1812, but another copy was discovered in 1864.

well as in original similes and symbols. The tie between Man and Nature is particularly profound. Thus Igor is helped in his flight by birds and trees. Rivers, plains, winds and forests seem to live one life with men. Certain passages, such as the laments of Igor's wife, are poignant in their dynamic simplicity."* Borodin, too, must have been deeply impressed by them, for his libretto preserves the original words and they struck out of him some of the most moving music he ever wrote.

Such was the poem with which Borodin lived for eighteen years, as Beethoven lived with the "Ode to Joy" for thirty, and Goethe with the Faust legend all his life. In order that his "Igor" should be accurate in every detail, the composer undertook extensive researches. History, archæology, folk-music—all were ransacked and every pertinent fragment carefully studied, so that not merely the superficial atmosphere of the time should be reproduced but its essential spirit made, as far as possible, to live again. And in Borodin the spirit of that old barbarism of the vast steppes and their nomadic warriors did live again. He was naturally adapted to receive and transmit such impressions; the

* **Janko Lavrin.**

descendant of princes—Caucasian princes—he betrayed both in his personal appearance and in many pages of even his earliest important composition, the E flat Symphony, the heroic and the Oriental elements in his nature. Yet nothing demonstrates more clearly the force of the impact on his mind of the "Song of Igor's Expedition" than the difference between the First Symphony and the Second. Borodin's musical talent lent itself most readily to purely lyrical expression; it was only the subject of "Igor" and the attendant researches that fired the talent to moments of genius and seemingly armed it with a new technique of utterance, almost terrible in its directness. The epic of Igor led this nineteenth century scientist back to primitive things—the natural, the physical, the cruel, the healthy. Almost all his later music glorifies them. An idea lived with for eighteen years must necessarily become part of a man, and if the world of "Prince Igor" was only a world of escape from the Academy of Medicine and the lectures on chemistry and the feminist campaign, it was probably more real to Borodin than this other more tangible world of science and sociology.

Borodin captured the spirit of "Igor" so miraculously that the weakness of the dramatic substance in which it is embodied seems at first sight the more deplorable. Igor, Prince of Seversk, sets out to punish a tribe of eastern nomads, is defeated and taken prisoner with his son—and escapes. That is the whole of the essential stuff of the drama, it would seem; the remaining action that pads out the prologue and the four acts of "Prince Igor" appears to be almost extraneous. Igor's brother-in-law stirs up trouble in his absence, but he disappears before the end of the first act; the disorder he causes merely provides a pretext for a stage-picture, just as the Polovtsian dances do at the end of the second act. There is a love-affair in Acts II and III between Igor's son and the daughter of one of the Polovtsian *khans*. It is used to heighten the excitement of Igor's escape, but otherwise the love interest seems to be introduced as pointlessly and arbitrarily as the comic interest, the rather childish clowning of the two gudok-players.* Nor

*Buffoons like Eroshka and Skula are stock-figures of classical Russian opera. We find them not only in avowedly comic works like "May Night" and "Christmas Eve" but in epic, fantastic and historical operas—in "Boris" (the drunken monks), in "Snegurochka" (Bobyl and Bobylicka), in "Sadko" (Duda and Sopiel). And Grishka Kuterma in "Kitezh" is just such another—seen tragically. But Eroshka and Skula were the prototypes. They were introduced into "Igor" by Borodin himself

is it an entirely satisfactory explanation to assume that the things we actually see and hear are really employed only to mirror those parts of the story of Igor's own adventures which cannot be shown at first hand on the stage. "Prince Igor" is, in fact, not so much a drama with personal protagonists as a series of scenes from an epic. So little was Borodin himself concerned with the dramatic element in his work that it was found, when he died, that he had never troubled to prepare a scenario, much less a finished libretto, for the second and third acts.

Yet before we finally dismiss "Prince Igor" as undramatic let us be quite clear as to what we mean by "drama" and "dramatic." In common usage the word "dramatic" has been so far degraded as to have become equivalent to "startling"; on a higher plane, we speak of the drama played out by the two principal subjects of a sonata-movement. In any case an element of contrast and clash is connoted and "Prince Igor," therefore, seems to be merely strewn with disconnected fragments of drama. But there is an antithesis which pervades

---

and, alluding to their disproportionate prominence, he jokingly remarked more than once that the opera would be more correctly entitled, not "Prince Igor," but "The Gudok-Players."

the whole work, the antithesis symbolised by the Russian elements in the music of the Prologue and Acts I and IV and the Polovtsian in that of Acts II and III—the clash between Slav and Tartar. Yet if the subject of the opera contains very little material of the type we are accustomed to think of as the proper stuff of drama, it is, nevertheless, a subject that not only provides an admirable pretext for stage-pictures but which can be presented by such pictures more effectively than by any other means. And the pictures are in every case of such a kind that music not merely *carries* them and heightens their effect but adds a new dimension, without which they would be incomplete. That fact alone, it seems to me, amply justifies the making of an opera on such a subject. Our emotions are stirred, not by sympathy with any of the characters (except perhaps Yaroslavna—who, in any case, is off the stage for two whole acts) or by a conflict of wills or ideas, but by the combined sensuous appeal of colour, sound and movement. The cumulative effect of all these detached scenes is out of all proportion to their effect taken separately. When they have passed, though passages like the choral dances and the unaccompanied chorus in Act IV may linger as high lights in the memory, one is left with a distinct impression of a rounded whole, complete and single. The spirit is too strong for the stuff in which it is embedded. For a few hours we watch these pictures of Russia's heroic age, while our receptive faculties, our imagination and our sensitiveness to impressions are quickened as only music can quicken them. The fate of Igor (who, like many another hero, is merely a lay-figure) scarcely interests us at all, but the re-created world in which he so signally fails to live abounds in life—and communicates a sense of that life to us. The real subject of the opera, it cannot be emphasised too strongly, is not a hero and his adventures but the spirit of a people and a period.

We must accept "Prince Igor," therefore, not as a musical drama but as a musical epic, a concert with action and costumes. That is to say, we must be content to allow it to affect us in the same way that concert-music does. But obviously the stage-setting is essential. An actual concert version of "Prince Igor" would be as ineffective as a concert version of "Tannhäuser" or "Figaro." Let us look then at the actual musical stuff of "Igor" for a moment, always keeping in mind the fact that its function is to increase our sensitiveness to pictures rather than to underline a drama. But Borodin never accompanies his stage-pictures, as Wagner was so fond of doing, with tautological translations of them into sound. The picture speaks for itself —*qua* picture; the music, retaining its tremendous advantage over the other arts of being able to transmit emotion purely, nakedly and directly, simply gives the emotional content of the picture. Or, conversely, one might say that the happenings on the stage illustrate the music. The music is the subject, the action and the picture the objective manifestation. The music seldom comments on, and never analyses, either drama or characters. In this respect " Prince Igor " is as far removed from " Boris Godunov " as " Boris " is from " Tristan."

The vocal lines in " Igor " are either frankly melodic or modelled on Dargomïzhsky's " melodic recitative." That is : the recitatives are to be *sung*, are, in fact, really *ariosi*. A direction at one point in Yaroslavna's long recitative in the fourth act is highly significant—*avec une grande émotion et presque déclamé*. Borodin was fully conscious of the pre-eminently lyrical nature of his opera : " From the dramatic point of view I have always been unlike the majority. Recitative does not enter into my nature or disposition. Although according to some critics I do not handle it altogether badly, I am far more attracted to melody and cantilena." And he goes on to mention a quality in which lies a great part of the secret of "Igor's" effectiveness: "I am drawn to definite and concrete forms. In opera, as in decorative art, details and *minutiæ* are out of place. Bold outlines only are necessary; all should be clear and straightforward and fit for practical performance from the vocal and instrumental standpoint. The voices should occupy the first place, the orchestra the second. I am no judge of the way in which I shall succeed, but my opera will be nearer akin to 'Ruslan' than to 'The Stone Guest.'" That was literally a confession of heresy, for, as we have seen, Dargomïzhsky's "Stone Guest" was known among the members of the "Kuchka" as "the Gospel."

So we find in Borodin's score set-numbers like Vladimir's cavatina and Igor's aria in Act II, as well as conventional choruses, sometimes frankly detached from the context, sometimes connected arbitrarily and without continuity of musical thought. Mingled with stretches of melodic recitative are purely melodic phrases, even snatches of formal, balanced melody (as in Yaroslavna's arioso, Act I, second tableau). Here one finds the indefinite outlines of lyrical recitative, supported on a shapeless background of chord melting into chord; there the very clear-cut melodic shapes of folk-music. Sometimes an actual folk-melody is employed, as in the unaccompanied chorus of peasants in Act IV—but on this ground one must tread cautiously, for the score contains no indications as to what material is of folk-origin and what is original. Instead of borrowing from existing collections, Borodin carried out folk-song researches on his own account* (the lovely melody of the peasants' chorus was one of his discoveries) and we have no means of determining the precise nature of the relationship of many of the "Prince Igor" melodies to actual folk-material. On the whole it is probably more spiritual than material, for Borodin had obviously absorbed the idiom and, in using it, reproduced the actual shapes of folk-music only subconsciously. This is true more particularly of the "Russian"

* According to Stassov, he also received from friends "some motives from songs of the Turkish races," motives noted by an explorer in Central Asia, and some musical material acquired from actual descendants of the Polovtsy now settled in a certain district in Hungary.

music; in the case of the "Polovtsian," which contrasts so sharply with it, one may venture to probe with a little more certainty into Borodin's treatment of his raw material. But the rather fascinating little problems to which this examination gives rise may be more conveniently dealt with later in considering Borodin's employment of the leit-motif.

The use of the leit-motif in "Prince Igor" is rudimentary—dramatic, for the sake of making points, rather than systematic as with Wagner. Yet it helps to disguise the varying style and uneven quality of the music, and the interruption of its continuity by the conventional set-numbers, by stamping it with at least a suggestion of material unity equivalent to the unquestionable unity (or rather, perhaps, Slav-Tartar duality) of its general feeling. Of personal leit-motifs, used on Wagnerian lines in strict association with a character and never failing to appear in connection with him, there are only two—that associated with Ovlur, the Christian Polovtsian who assists Igor to escape, and the striking theme of falling diminished fifths heard when the Khan, Konchak, first enters in the second act and throughout the remainder of Acts II and III. The "Ovlur" theme is employed much less frequently and purely for dramatic emphasis. It is used throughout the scene in which the traitor first approaches Igor with the offer to help him to escape (and some of the solemn Prologue music is heard as the captive Prince's thoughts turn to his people; it calls attention to him as he crosses the stage with *kumïs* for the guards in Act III; and it is used, with some of the other music heard during his previous interview with Igor, in the ensuing scene where he tells the Prince that all is ready for the flight. But here again we are confronted with a doubt which it is difficult to resolve with certainty. Not only is a great deal of the music of this scene between Igor and Ovlur drawn from that of their discussion in Act II, but much of the music of the preceding scene with the guards is also based on material previously used, the quotation of which here can have no dramatic significance. Borodin may have intended by this means to draw the threads of his work a little closer, but we must not forget that he left his opera unfinished and that Glazunov, to whom the completion and orchestration of this third act was entrusted,* may have preferred to make use of

* Glazunov also wrote out the overture "nearly according to

Borodin's own themes for the filling up of *lacunæ* rather than to incorporate fresh material of his own in the master's work. This is certainly the case in the Finale of the act, which we know was almost entirely composed by Glazunov. On the other hand the quotations from Igor's big aria in Act II (when he tells Konchak that if he were free he would renew the war and not make peace "till he had drawn water from the Don in his helmet"; when Vladimir, in Act III, is hesitating between love and duty; and during Yaroslavna's lament in Act IV) are dramatically significant and very effective. Then again there is some interesting play of motives in the early scenes where Galitsky is prominent. The music of his brief assurance of fidelity to Igor in the Prologue ironically provides the material for two fairly long passages in the first act, when his

Borodin's plan," having frequently heard the composer play it on the piano, and scored it. The remainder of "Prince Igor," including the Polovtsian March in Act III, was orchestrated by Rimsky-Korsakov. We also owe the music of the beautiful little chorus of Russian prisoners in Act II to Glazunov's memory; the words and Konchakovna's introductory recitative were added by Rimsky-Korsakov. It is characteristic of Glazunov's modesty that he has destroyed the "legend" that he "wrote out the Overture entirely from memory." Actually, of course, the material all existed in the body of the opera. Glazunov also refuses to "guarantee the precise accuracy" of the chorus of prisoners.

treachery has been fully revealed; a tumultuous quaver passage is three times associated with him; and there is a striking "Hail, Prince Galitsky" motif, first sung by the basses, which is afterwards developed at considerable length in the final chorus of the first tableau of Act I ("Let us place him on the throne"). The last four pages of this scene, again, pass in review much that has gone before, rounding it off as a compact musical whole, though in no way illuminating the dramatic action.

Still more interesting are the themes associated with the Polovtsy; and in discussing these we are led back to a subject already touched on, the nature of Borodin's treatment of the raw material he had gathered. The Polovtsian, the oriental, element dominates the music of the second and third acts, and Act II plunges us at once into the new atmosphere with a striking chorus of Polovtsian girls. Four typical phrases of its strangely haunting melody are here quoted separately for convenience of reference :—

Ex. 28.

Their relationship to each other is sufficiently obvious. None is a variation of another; all are, as it were, different aspects of the same idea. It will be noticed that the features common to these fragments are strongly distinctive and therefore of such a type that they naturally give a peculiar stamp to any melody in which they appear. Whether the whole long extended melody of this chorus* is a genuine Tartar tune or whether Borodin manufactured it from such fragments as the initial motif of (a), (b) and (d), the falling triplet of (a), (c) and (d), and so on, it is impossible to say with certainty. But it is clearly either genuine raw material or material in only the first stage of manufacture. Either Borodin got most of his "Polovtsian" clichés from this tune or he took this opportunity of making a synthesis of nearly all the melodic and rhythmic features he had observed to be characteristic of the folk-music he wished to imitate; and of the two, the former seems decidedly the more reasonable supposition. With the next step, the tracing of Borodin's "culture" of these germ-themes, we reach firm ground—and incidentally discover what

* The other melodic shapes are similarly related to these but, being inessential to the discussion, are not quoted.

gives the music of these two acts its *cachet* of unity.

Of the four fragments of Ex. 28, (d) is by far the most important. We recognise it again first as the generating theme of Konchakovna's cavatina,* "Night, falling quickly":—

Ex. 29.

The new feature, the appoggiatura emphasising the triplet, is important and characteristic. The fragment, "I wait for thee":—

Ex. 30.

with the little pendant (to "zhdu tebya"), is also heard in the orchestra in this number, and was again quoted by Rimsky-Korsakov in a pause in the brief recitative for Konchakovna introducing the following chorus of Russian prisoners.

Konchak's big aria later in the act is based, not

* The cavatina has a choral accompaniment *not* by Borodin. The chorus-parts were added gratuitously by Rimsky-Korsakov after the composer's death.

immediately on Ex. 28 (d), but on the variation Ex. 29 (or rather on the "spuskaïsya" part of it), with the appoggiatura notes now broadened into an essential part of the melodic line ("No, no, friend. No prince, thou art not my prisoner here"):—

Ex. 31.

An accompaniment-figure :—

Ex. 32.

used later, is more directly derived from Ex. 28 (d). The brief, quick orchestral coda of the aria preserves the melodic shape of the first three bars of Ex. 31, but a fresh appoggiatura is inserted before the triplet. From the new figure thus obtained is developed the music of Yaroslavna's lament which opens Act IV :—

Ex. 33.

The further transformations of Ex. 31 in the Finale of Act III are apparently Glazunov's. The adventures of Ex. 28 (b) are less striking, but a variation :—

Ex. 34.

plays an important part in the famous dances at the end of Act II.

Ex. 28 (c) is particularly interesting, for it is marked by what is perhaps the most personal of all Borodin's melodic mannerisms, one so peculiar to him and occurring so frequently in his music that it almost has the effect of placing his signature to any melody in which it is found. We find it in the opening of the B minor Symphony (Ex. 1)—and the working-out gives it much additional prominence; in the chief subject of the finale of the Second String Quartet; and, inverted, in the opening of the Symphony in E flat (Ex. 19). In "Prince Igor" it occurs in passage-work, in the melody to which the curtain rises on the second tableau of Act I, in Igor's great aria (Act II) in the Polovtsian dances and on a dozen other pages of the score.

The binding effect of such constantly recurring motives, in music otherwise diffuse and disconnected, is surprisingly strong, the more so perhaps because they are comparatively unobtrusive. And in a slightly different way the triumphal fanfare of the Polovtsian March, which is heard again and again throughout the third act, to which the curtain rises and on which it falls, seems to frame and, if the idea be not too fanciful, throw into relief the rest of the music of that act. It also recalls a passage in the B minor Symphony, forcibly drawing one's attention to the fact that there are material as well as spiritual links between the two works. The resemblances between the second subject of the first movement of the symphony (Ex. 26) and the final *marziale* chorus of "Igor" are not less significant because they are accidental. A motif from one of the choruses of Act I is used in the finale of the symphony. And in "On the Steppes of Central Asia" also (where again the central idea is the musical contrasting of Slav and Tartar) one easily recognises the derivation of the *cor anglais* melody from Ex. 28 (a) and (d). If the B minor Symphony was an idealisation of the best of the material gathered for the composition of "Igor," "On the Steppes of

Central Asia" was clearly made of chips from the same workship. And we know that the trio of the Third Symphony was actually based on material originally intended for the opera (the merchant's account of Igor's defeat, which was originally intended to form part of the finale of Act I).

VIII.—RIMSKY-KORSAKOV'S FIRST OPERA.

IN November, 1865, at the outset of his career as a composer, Rimsky-Korsakov wrote his first song, a setting of Heine's "Lehn deine Wang' an meine Wang.'" Balakirev, whose influence over the younger man was at that time absolute, approved of the melody but condemned the accompaniment as unpianistic and characteristically wrote a fresh one, with which the song was published. In the following spring, incited by the singing of a certain Madame Zotova, whom he had met at the house of Glinka's sister, Rimsky-Korsakov wrote three more songs, this time with his own accompaniments, and all four were soon after published together as his Opus 2. One of the songs was another Heine setting, "Aus meinen Tränen spriessen" (a poem which also seduced Borodin into unsuccessful competition with Schumann), one the well-known "The Rose enslaves the Nightingale," and the third a setting of the cradle-song in the first act of Leo Mey's drama, "Pskovityanka" ("The Maid of Pskov"). That was Rimsky-Korsakov's first encounter with a work which was to occupy him at intervals for a quarter of a century, of which indeed the last note was not written till 1899, when he inserted in the last act of his opera an additional—or, rather, alternative—aria for Chaliapin as the Tsar.

The idea of turning Mey's play into an opera was born several months later than the song. It originated with Balakirev and Mussorgsky. From the very beginning the first act was seen to offer serious difficulties. Its action takes place fifteen years before the rest of the play and is concerned with quite a different set of characters. It serves only to explain the secret of the heroine's parentage, yet without this clue the drama is hardly a comprehensible whole. The solution adopted by Rimsky-Korsakov and his informal advisory committee, to omit the first act altogether and give the gist of it in a dialogue in the third, was the only possible one. But it never satisfied even the composer himself. "The question of a librettist," he tells us incidentally, "never arose. It was taken for granted that I should have to write the 'book' myself."

For the time being the thought of an opera was

thrust aside by the composition of "Antar." Then in the summer of 1868 came genuine inspiration, provoked by an invitation to visit a musical friend, with whom the Borodins were staying, whose estate was in the Tver Government. The invitation reached the composer in his brother's empty town house and the prospect of a journey into the heart of Russia awoke in him "a sudden, extremely powerful feeling of love for the Russian people, for their history in general and for 'Pskovityanka' in particular." And under the influence of this passionate emotion he improvised at the piano the theme of the chorus with which the people greet Tsar Ivan. During this country holiday he watched the dances of the peasants, and on his return to Petersburg wrote, evidently under the influence of these impressions, the music of the opening scene where the girls are singing and playing in Prince Tokmakov's garden. The tale of the Tsarevna Lada was written at the same time. Then another external event occurred to modify the course of the composition of "Pskovityanka." In the first days of 1869 Dargomïzhsky died and, in accordance with his wishes, his unfinished "Stone Guest" was handed over to Cui to finish and to

CUI.

Rimsky-Korsakov to orchestrate. The scoring of "The Stone Guest" and the composition of "Pskovityanka" went on side by side, a fact which partially accounts for the exceptionally dramatic tendency of the latter. Both works progressed slowly; Rimsky-Korsakov was still a naval officer, and his duties, though not exacting, took up much time. A heavier hindrance to the work was the composer's astounding ignorance of the technique of composition. He was in the position of a Robinson Crusoe, a workman without tools. On his own confession, he was unable at that time to harmonise a simple chorale properly; he had "only a hazy idea of fugue"; and his "ideas of musical form were very confused." Instinct and a good ear were his only guides; he had an unconscious feeling for good part-writing; and he could distinguish without the least difficulty every note in each chord. But the only chords he knew by name were the major and minor triads and the dominant and diminished sevenths; he had never heard of "six-four" chords. It was the same with his orchestration; like Berlioz he scored colourfully by instinct from the beginning. Just as the Frenchman had written "Les Franc-Juges" without knowing whether it could be played, the composer of "Sadko" and "Antar" had no thorough knowledge of the technique even of the strings! The writing of an opera was a truly heroic feat for a composer with such equipment, though Mussorgsky did the whole of his life-work with very little better. But Rimsky-Korsakov was not content to play the "inquisitive savage discovering music step by step." He saw how quickly his creative fantasy was brought to a standstill for want of fresh methods of treatment. In his own expressive phrase, the acquisition of a technique "freed his hands." But the delightful spectacle of the Professor of Free Composition at the Petersburg Conservatoire conscientiously working figured basses and harmonising simple melodies was reserved for the year 1874; the whole of "Pskovityanka" in its original form was the work of a complete musical ignoramus. The scoring of "The Stone Guest" was finished in the summer of 1870* and its immediate influence was replaced by another. Various circumstances, principally the illness of the

* Many years afterwards Rimsky-Korsakov, dissatisfied with his treatment of Dargomizhsky's masterpiece, orchestrated it entirely afresh, and at the same time smoothed out, in his usual editorial manner, the "harmonic crudities of the original." This second version was completed in 1902.

brother with whom he had been living, led to Rimsky-Korsakov's sharing rooms with Mussorgsky, and the two men worked at the same writing-table, one finishing his "Pskovityanka" while the other was composing and orchestrating additional scenes (the Polish act and the scene in the forest near Kromy being the most important) for "Boris Godunov," in the hope that its new form would induce the directorate of the Imperial Opera to reconsider their refusal to produce it. There were serious interruptions to the composition of "Pskovityanka"—the death of the composer's brother in November, with a consequent journey to Italy to bring home the body, and the composer's betrothal in December—but the score was finished by January, 1872.

With "Pskovityanka" began Rimsky-Korsakov's troubles with the dramatic censorship, troubles which intermittently attended his career as an operatic composer right up to the banning of "The Golden Cockerel." The censor objected to the scene of the "veche," the parliament of the free citizens of Pskov, which in the sixteenth century was still a member of the Hanseatic League and practically an independent republic. The Tsarist government would not tolerate the stage representation of a republican institution, and the perfectly legal "veche" had to be turned into an assembly of rebels. An even more serious difficulty, a ukase of Nicholas I forbidding the introduction of members of the Romanov dynasty as characters in opera (though not in ordinary drama), was circumvented by backstairs methods,* and Rimsky-Korsakov at last had the satisfaction of seeing his work produced in January, 1873, with considerable success.

But his satisfaction was short-lived. The well-equipped technician who emerged from the contrapuntal crisis of 1874 was heartily ashamed of the crudities of his score. "I was conscious of the harmonic extravagances, the disconnectedness of the recitative, the want of sustained melody . . . and the absence of contrapuntal elements." He was dissatisfied also with the scoring—the "senseless choice of natural horns and trumpets" (two horns in F, two in C, and trumpets in C), the ineffective string-writing and the absence of any sonorous *forte*. Balakirev also pressed for the revision of

* Tchaïkovsky was less fortunate with his "Oprichnik" a few months later. Ivan the Terrible was also to have appeared in this opera, but the censor insisted on the excision of the part.

"Pskovityanka," on the ground that Rimsky-Korsakov was unlikely to write another opera and that it was therefore his duty to make the best of his first-born. Accordingly in 1876 the conscientious composer set about not a mere revision but an entire re-writing of the work. He now set Mey's first act as a prologue, introducing his Op. 2, No. 3, Vera's cradle-song, and made other additions—among them, at Balakirev's demand, a chorus of those begging pilgrims who form such a large proportion of the floating population of Russian opera. The work was also entirely re-orchestrated, but once more, curiously enough, with natural brass "although the harmonies and modulations imperatively demanded valve instruments." But the second version of "Pskovityanka" pleased nobody, not even the composer himself. It suffered from excess of technical ingenuity even more than the first version had done from lack of it. The additions made the work too long and destroyed its unity of style, and Rimsky-Korsakov had to admit that he had strangled his music in a web of counterpoint. The Imperial Theatres would not produce the opera in its new form; so, despairing of seeing it on the stage, Rimsky-Korsakov again re-scored the new "miniature overture" to the prologue, and the entr'actes, this time with chromatic brass, and issued them as a concert suite "like the music to 'Prince Kholmsky' or 'Egmont.'"

In the spring of 1891 Rimsky-Korsakov heroically began a second complete revision. So far was he from tamely accepting Weber's dictum that "first operas are like first puppies, only fit to be drowned." This time he determined to follow the first version for the most part, only drawing on the second to replace completely unsuccesful passages; the new orchestration was "partly according to Glinka's principles, partly on Wagnerian lines," with triple wood-wind instead of in pairs as before. Among other changes, the overture was transposed from B minor to C minor, completely re-scored, and "the barbaric dissonances at the end replaced by more respectable music." This final version of the opera was finished in 1894, just before the composition of "Christmas Eve," and produced in the following year. The prologue, which had been omitted from the third version, was also brushed up in the spring of 1898 and published as a self-contained one-act opera, "Boyarina Vera Sheloga." Few operas can have had a more eventful history, but in spite of this bewildering succession of re-births we can still accept "Pskovityanka" as Rimsky-Korsakov's first opera. The earlier versions are not available for comparison, but Yastrebtsev, who played Boswell to Rimsky-Korsakov's Johnson, confirms the composer's statement that the final version is for the most part simply a revision of the first. And the internal evidence makes such confirmation almost unnecessary. Not only "Pskovityanka" but the First and Third Symphonies, the so-called "Second Symphony" ("Antar"), the orchestral "Sadko," the "Fantasia on Serbian Themes"—in fact, all Rimsky-Korsakov's important compositions prior to "May Night"—underwent similar revision in later years, so that a critic of the early Rimsky-Korsakov is liable to be tripped up at every step. Fortunately criticism of "Pskovityanka" is simplified by the facts that the music is subordinated to the drama and that the dramatic outline was left practically unchanged.

If anyone wants to see exactly what Dargomïzhsky and the younger Russians of the time were aiming at in opera, without choking himself with dust from the dry bones of "The Stone Guest" or bewildering himself with Mussorgsky's genius in

"Boris," he cannot do better than study "Pskovityanka." Rimsky-Korsakov was conscientious above all else; he was just the man to write a "model" opera. His own inclinations, like Borodin's, seem to have been towards lyrical opera in Glinka's style, except that his lyrical vein was alloyed with a strongly fantastic element which appears only occasionally in Glinka and not at all in Borodin. Yet he must needs try his hand at dramatic realism in the orthodox Dargomïzhskian manner for which he had no real gift—though, unconvinced on this point, he returned to it in "Mozart and Salieri" and "Vera Sheloga." So in "Pskovityanka" we find the famous "melodic recitative" used almost throughout (though the "melodic" qualification is not unduly emphasised) and an absence of conventional set-numbers, except the interpolated aria for the Tsar in the last act and Olga's arietta in Act II, Scene I, which was inserted in the second version in place of an *arioso* in the first. On the other hand, a number of passages can easily be detached from the context and performed as self-contained numbers. The folk-song element is well to the fore—real (as the song of the rebels, Olga's pleading "Stay with me, my love" in the first act, and the lovely melody which accompanies the dialogue of the nurses in the opening scene) and imitated (as the song Tucha sings when he first comes striding over the fence into Prince Tokmakov's garden). And the chorus, the voice of the people of Pskov, is the most impressive protagonist in the drama until—an effective point—the appearance of the Tsar himself.

The alternative title of the opera, "Ivan the Terrible," was adopted by Dyaghilev as a concession to the linguistic difficulties of Western audiences. But it is perhaps on the whole more fitting than the original one. It is true the opera is concerned with the love and death of Olga, the Maid of Pskov, but her part in the drama is an almost purely passive one. The central figure is her father, the Tsar. At first it appears as if the real subject of the drama is to be the struggle between the Tsar and the citizens of Pskov, the same subject as in "Boris"—the struggle between a tyrant and the will of the people. But whereas in "Boris" the centre of dramatic gravity remains in this contest (the revelation of Boris's agony being, after all, only incidental), in "Pskovityanka" this issue drops into the background with the love-affair of Olga and Tucha, and the main drama is seen to be that of the warring elements in Ivan's own soul. Viewed in this light "Pskovityanka" appears as one long-drawn dramatic crescendo, of which the full significance is revealed only at the end. Ivan himself does not appear till half-way through the second act, more than half-way through the whole opera, but everything that precedes his entrance is like the gradual gathering of his shadow. He is first mentioned by the nurses during the light-hearted songs and games of the girls in the opening scene; but Vlassevna's brief account of the sack of Novgorod hardly interrupts the general feeling of merriment. His shadow grows more distinct in the dialogue between Tokmakov and Matuta. And in both conversations his relationship to Olga is dimly hinted at. Now, when Tokmakov, not daring to tell the truth, says, "But her father we know not," the Tsar's theme is heard in the orchestra for the first time—a curious instance of a potentially dramatic effect thrown away, for the motif, afterwards so effective, is at this point not yet clothed with association and is therefore meaningless to anyone hearing the work for the first time. The conversation is interrupted by the ringing of the alarm-bell,* and its tolling—which continues without interruption throughout the rest of the scene, the ensuing intermezzo and the gathering of the people, right up to the great choral cry to the messenger from Novgorod, "Yes, let him speak"—creates an atmosphere of tension, the sense of an overhanging doom, intensified by the finely conceived choruses of which the rest of the act consists. Tokmakov tries to soothe the people; Tucha inflames them. But it is the chorus, the voice of the people themselves, uttering their fears, their doubts, their submission or their defiance, which dominates everything. Nothing could be more profoundly impressive than the conclusion when, after the song of the rebels has died away and the bells are tolling again for the summoning of the "veche," those left on the stage murmur that "the end draws near. The Tsar is wrath." In the broad, falling phrases of the chorus seem to be concentrated both the awe of the particular moment and the essence of that passive, mournful submission to an invincible destiny which is at once the tragedy and the salvation of the Russian soul.

The chorus again dominates the whole of the first

* Suggested by overtones, as in the "Overture on Russian Themes" of 1866.

scene of the second act, where the Tsar is immediately expected, and the tension is again drawn to a gradual climax which reaches its extreme point when the Tsar rides in and—another most effective point—the curtain falls immediately. The shadow has now become substance; though, paradoxically, the substance owes all its formidable authority to the shadow, the dread which the Tsar's name has been seen to inspire.

Up to this point the composer has been able to get along very well with purely musical means—appeals to the people and big, exciting choruses. Now he has to show Ivan himself and to show him so that he justifies the general terror so elaborately painted. Rimsky-Korsakov really plays his cards very well. Having a poor hand in his own natural gifts, he plays up to his partner, the dramatist, so well that between them they make trick after trick. Even the interlude which bridges the gap between the crowded scene in the market-place and the first close-up of the Tsar in Tokmakov's house shows some sense of the theatre. As a concert piece this quiet meditation on the naïve themes associated with

Olga would fall rather flat; here, as a point of repose between two dramatic scenes, it not only throws what follows into higher relief but is extremely effective in itself.

The scene in Tokmakov's house needs no music to make it effective. The character of the half-mad Tsar reveals itself stroke by stroke: in his quibbling, "To enter or not? . . . I'll enter if the grace of God Almighty and His blessing rest upon this house"; in his ironical pretence that he cannot even sit down without Tokmakov's permission; in his thanks ao Tokmakov and Matuta, his "two devoted courtiers . . . on the right an angel, on the left a devil! They're silent . . . yet each one plots in himself. Well, though I'm but an idiot, aye, and a miscreant, God's most sinful servant, I'll judge ye both if God but wills it so."* Rimsky-Korsakov's mezzo-recitative is no more than a vehicle for the words, and the orchestral background entirely woven from the Tsar's motif in imitation and in different registers, is not at all expressive; yet somehow this cold, serenely royal back-

* I have followed Mrs. Newmarch's translation of the libretto throughout. (Bessel Edition: for which Boosey and Hawkes are the English agents.)

ground—for it is emphatically background and not commentary—throws the figure of the Tsar into striking relief. Consider, for instance, his outburst when Tokmakov hails him as "Tsar! Gossudar!"—

Ex. 35.

But even the moment when Ivan recognises Olga as his daughter fails to strike genuinely dramatic music out of Rimsky-Korsakov; he takes refuge in convention—soft, slow chords, a quiet harp arpeggio, and then an agitated version of the Tsar's theme in quick time. The convention is adequate to the occasion; but one cannot help feeling that Mussorgsky would have written something that was more than adequate. Rimsky-Korsakov clearly did not *feel* such situations and one is very conscious that he is happy to pass on to Olga's simple lyrical reply and of the relief with which he evades the point musically by dragging in a folk-songish girls' chorus as a background to the rest of the conversation. Separation of the musical and dramatic centres of gravity in this fashion was an ever-present help in time of trouble to Rimsky-Korsakov.

The third act begins by wandering among irrelevancies—the picturesque but quite unnecessary "Tsar's Hunt and Storm," so obviously imitated from Berlioz's "Troyens," introduced in the final version of the opera, the beautiful unison folk-song chorus of the girls looking for Olga, and the extraordinarily passionless love-duet, a wilderness of even crotchets in 5/4 time. But when the curtain rises on the second scene, revealing the Tsar alone in his tent, the drama reaches its height. We have seen the growing shadow of Ivan's dreaded coming, the terror of his reputation; we have seen the man himself and his behaviour to those about him. And now finally the whole of his tortured soul is laid bare to us, like Boris Godunov's, and at last Rimsky-Korsakov is moved to music of real dramatic power and psychological subtlety. It is impossible to believe that Rimsky-Korsakov wrote this scene without some thought of Boris, whose tragic history, as we have seen, was being re-shaped during the composition of "Pskovityanka." And it is something more than a coincidence that Chaliapin became the outstanding interpreter of both parts. Rimsky-Korsakov's admiration for this "incomparable Ivan the Terrible" led him into a curious error of judgment, the insertion of the aria already mentioned, a piece written in the insipid style of the weakest pages of "The Tsar's Bride," after the Tsar's first words, "Well, I have pardoned Pskov, but the girl still haunts my memory." It is not only that the brooding phrases of the orchestra in the original version (Ex. 36), seem to lose their "edge" and character when transferred to the voice; the whole thing is foreign to the world of dramatic realism in terms of which the scene was conceived in the first place. Now the Tsar's thoughts turn to Vera, Olga's mother, and his declamation is broken while the orchestra seems to dream as he half whispers to himself, "The past uprises: the wood, the orchard, she herself . . . I saw her, and my heart throbbed past endurance.

Ex. 36.

. . . And now the fruit tastes bitter." Then he recalls his royal mission, as he conceives it: "Aye, but that kingdom's strongest, greatest, most invincible, in which the people know that in one man the power is vested, a single flock gathered around one shepherd." The vision of a holy autocracy reaches its climax:—

Ex. 37.

And then comes doubt again: "But will the Lord then grant me strength and wisdom?" He turns the pages of his missal, reading the divine commands "to punish rebels, and make an end of evildoers and sinners; Thou giv'st Thy disciples power to destroy and to crush out scorpions and serpents and to overcome all the forces of the Evil One. . . ." And then, after one of those silences which the stilling of music makes so impressive, the terrible sigh, "Oh, I am sad."

In these pages Rimsky-Korsakov really reaches the highest point of his achievement as a dramatic realist. Nowhere else in the whole range of his work, except perhaps in the music of Grishka Kuterma in "Kitezh," is there anything comparable with this probing of the mysteries of abnormal psychology. It was not his *métier*. And, knowing that, one feels the added exhilaration one always gets from the spectacle of a man doing something unnatural to him and doing it rather well. Ivan's portrait is not yet complete; we have still to see his ungovernable rage against Matuta, to see him playing cat and mouse with the daughter he loves, incapable of kindness without an alloy of cruelty, masking fondness with irony, and finally to see him sobbing over her dead body, commanding her to listen—"'Tis I, the Tsar . . ."—and frantically imploring the physician, Bomelius, to save her, "my child, my darling." But poignant as is the music which accompanies the final tragedy, it cannot be compared in psychological truth with that of the Tsar's long soliloquy.

Beside this full-length study of the Tsar, the other characters are merely sketched, and his domination of the stage is thus given additional emphasis. But this emphasis is quite unnecessary on the one hand, while on the other it is obvious that the force of his personality is weakened by the lack of a suitable foil. For the most part he is contrasted with Olga, a rather colourless figure; colourless not because she is incompetently drawn, for the charmingly simple, lyrical music associated with her precisely reflects her naïve character, but because she *is* naïve, the first of those innocent, passive heroines who appear in so many of Rimsky--Korsakov's operas. No real daughter of Ivan the Terrible could have been quite as negative as Olga. But she belongs to a type we meet fairly often in Russian literature and which we must therefore assume to be a true portrait of a common type of Russian girlhood, a type which evidently appealed to Rimsky-Korsakov. Tokmakov, too, is negative by nature, and Rimsky-Korsakov contrived to outline his amiable, conciliatory character in such music as the chords which accompany his address to the people of Pskov and the phrase to which he sings, "I am growing old, Matuta," without lapsing into insipidity. On the other hand, Tucha who is positive, the typical rebel, the natural foil to the Tsar (though they never appear on the stage at the same time), is not really alive at all. Or, rather, he begins by being alive when he first comes on the stage with his song about the cuckoo, and gradually becomes more and more wooden. As for Matuta, he is nothing more than a lay-figure from beginning to end—and the mere outline of a lay-figure at that. He seems to have some importance not accounted for in the opera at all.

It is easier to grasp "Pskovityanka" as a dramatic whole than as a musical one. At a first hearing one is inclined to say that it is really typical of Rimsky-Korsakov in nothing but its folk-songish elements and perhaps in the somewhat dry and astringent quality of the harmony. Yet looking at it more closely, one finds in embryo practically all the constituents of the mature Rimsky-Korsakov's musical mentality. The germ of the whole of the fantastic Korsakov is to be found in the accompaniment to Vlassevna's tale of the Tsarevna Lada; for example, where in her description of the dragon Tugarin, she says that "his tail measures twenty-three yards at least":—

Ex. 38.

And her short recitative phrases, which so perfectly match the style of the popular Russian fairy-tales, are the first example of a very individual type of declamation one finds in Rimsky-Korsakov's later "fairy-tale" operas, in "Snegurochka" and above all in "Tsar Saltan" and "The Golden Cockerel," just as Tokmakov's:—

Ex. 39.

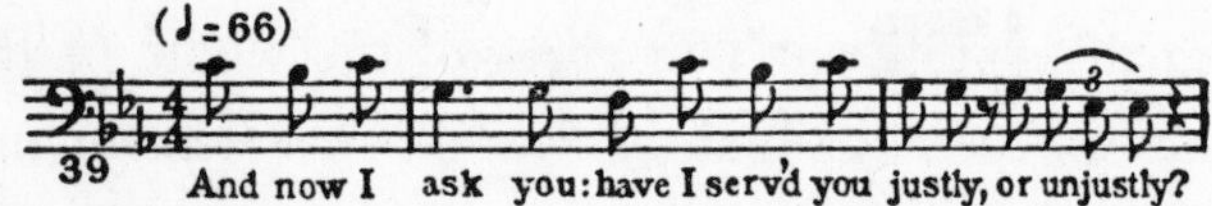

is premonitive of the peculiar "bïlina" declamation used systematically for the first time in "Sadko."

The composer's sensitiveness to the qualities and associative powers of different keys, which was only just beginning to awaken when he wrote the original version of "Pskovityanka," shows itself in the, possibly accidental, association of Tokmakov with E flat major. One notices, too, the progression of major chords on a bass in descending major thirds, when Tokmakov cries "Tsar, Gossudar, my homage!" and the descending major scale, with sharpened fourth, first heard when Olga begs Tucha not to leave her, which recurs like a dark shadow over their love later in the work. These points are not outstanding features of the score, but they are noteworthy because they are portents.

IX.—RIMSKY-KORSAKOV'S GOGOL OPERAS.

GOGOL made his literary début in 1831 with a volume of short stories called "Evenings on a Farm near Dikanka." They are tales of village life in his native Ukraine, based for the most part on Little Russian folk-lore, but fantastically and humorously embroidered by the writer's imagination. Historically the "Evenings" are important as the first specimens of finely wrought modern Russian prose. Indeed, Gogol's style in these early stories was almost too rich and ornamental; as one critic puts it, he was "often in danger of drugging himself with the sensuous aspects of words." The "Evenings on a Farm" hardly suggest the Gogol of "The Revizor" and "Dead Souls," but they are masterpieces of their kind—and they provide first-rate material for a certain type of musician.

The first composer to draw on the "Evenings" for operatic material was the now-almost-forgotten Alexander Serov. His choice fell on "Christmas

Eve," and a libretto was prepared for him by Polonsky, a poet whose position in Russian literature is roughly equivalent to Tennyson's in our own. But Serov died in 1871, with the music of "Christmas Eve" hardly begun, and the Imperial Russian Musical Society instituted a competition for the best setting of Polonsky's "book." Rimsky-Korsakov, Napravnik and Nicholas Rubinstein were among the members of the jury and the successful competitor was Tchaïkovsky—Serov's pupil, Solovev being awarded the second prize. Tchaïkovsky's opera, "Vakula the Smith," was produced at St. Petersburg in 1876. But the public took to "Vakula" less kindly than the judges had done, and Tchaïkovsky revised and re-christened the work more than once. After existing for a time as "Oxana's Caprice," it won success at last as "The Little Shoes." In the meantime two members of the "mighty handful" had also begun operas based on stories from the "Evenings on a Farm," and during the late 'seventies we find Mussorgsky and Rimsky Korsakov working simultaneously at "The Fair of Sorochintsy" and "May Night" respectively. Mussorgsky died with his "Fair" still in a very fragmentary state, but Rimsky-Korsakov's opera was quickly finished—much more quickly than the first version of "Pskovityanka." He had now conquered the mysteries of counterpoint, after writing a group of works—the String Quartet and Sextet, the Third Symphony, and the second version of "Pskovityanka"—in which it is clear that counterpoint had temporarily conquered him. The editing, with Balakirev, of the full scores of Glinka's operas had been his artistic salvation and in his second opera he threw overboard both dramatic realism and technique for technique's sake. Just as "Pskovityanka" is overshadowed by the theories of Dargomïzhsky, "May Night" is illuminated by Glinka's spirit.

Gogol's "Evenings" had had a warm corner in Rimsky-Korsakov's affections from the days of his childhood and "May Night" had always been his favourite tale. Later it acquired an additional sentimental value, for he and Nadezhda Purgold had read it together on the day of their betrothal in December, 1871, and it was that very sensible and thoroughly musical woman who persuaded him to make an opera of it. But, although musical ideas for the work had been accumulating for some years, it was not until February, 1878, that the composition was actually begun. And begun, curiously enough, with the third act, which Stassov and the composer himself rightly considered the best part of the work but which was the only part that displeased the singers. The score was finished in October of the same year; the piano version followed later—proof enough that instrumental colour formed an integral part of Rimsky-Korsakov's musical thought, even at this stage when he was still feeling his way as an orchestrator and writing "in Glinka's transparent style" for the old classical orchestra, with natural horns and trumpets. The opera, naturally dedicated to the composer's wife, was produced at the Imperial Theatre, Petersburg, in January, 1880, the scenery being that used for Tchaïkovsky's unlucky "Vakula," with December painted into May. Sixteen years later Rimsky-Korsakov again turned to the "Evenings," his choice this time falling on the favourite "Christmas Eve," which Tchaïkovsky's death had just "set free," as he put it. Only the fear of giving offence to Tchaïkovsky had prevented his setting "Christmas Eve" before. But he rejected Polonsky's "thoroughly unsatisfactory" libretto in favour of one of his own composition.

Rimsky-Korsakov was peculiarly well adapted to

interpret Gogol, at least the early Gogol of these tales. He had the same love of the fantastic and the naïvely humorous, and he loved sound for sound's sake very much as Gogol loved words. He followed his author very faithfully, even as regards dialogue, being content simply to put each story on the stage and clothe it with appropriate music, only underlining and filling out (particularly in the later opera) the fantastic parts and references to customs and beliefs derived from the old Slavonic mythology, which since 1875 had interested him so profoundly. That may not be the best way to write a musical drama, but it is not a bad method of turning out a jolly entertainment, and it was certainly the only way of getting Gogol inside an opera-house without taking away everything that makes him Gogol. (And, after all, even Verdi and Boïto knocked a good deal of the Shakespeare out of Shakespeare.)

The subjects of both operas are very similar. In both there are the same young peasants, the same village maidens, the same delightful, simple-minded old rascals of village dignitaries, involved in the same kind of broadly farcical situations, the same solution of the lover's difficulties by comic-supernatural means, and the same opportunities to introduce traditional choruses connected with the season—Whitsuntide in one case, Christmas in the other.* Levko, the hero of "May Night," cannot get his father, the *golova* or headman of the village, to consent to his marriage with his sweetheart, Hanna, and, finding that the old man is actually his rival, he avenges himself by egging on the other young Cossacks to play the wildest pranks on the *golova,* his sister-in-law and his friend, the village scribe. In the third act, Levko, dreaming by the lakeside, sees the russalkas or water-nymphs playing in the moonlight, and finds for them a witch who is troubling them. In gratitude their queen gives him a note which he is to hand to his father. At dawn the headman and scribe, with the watch, find him and, recognising the disguised ringleader of the rioters, are going to seize him—when he produces the letter. The scribe recognises the Commissary's writing and reads: "To the Headman, Eutychius Makogonenko. We hear

* Rimsky-Korsakov, probably rightly, saw in these Christian festivals little more than modern corruptions of the old rites connected with the vernal equinox and winter solstice. The pantheist in the nature-loving composer sympathised more with the ancient than with the modern forms of these ceremonies.

that you, like an old fool, instead of keeping order in the village, have been giving rise to scandal yourself. You are to permit the immediate marriage of your son, Levko Makogonenko, with the girl, Hanna Petritshenkova; likewise to repair the bridges on the post-road. If, on my arrival, I find these orders have not been obeyed, you alone will be held responsible. Commissary and retired Lieutenant, Kosma Derkatsh-Drishpantovsky." The comic-supernatural plays an even more important part in "Christmas Eve." The smith Vakula is in love with a coquettish beauty, Oxana, daughter of an old Cossack, Chub, but she only laughs at him—mockingly promising to marry him, however, if he will give her a pair of shoes like the Tsaritsa's. Now Vakula's mother, Solokha, is a witch whose numerous lovers include the Devil, the village headman, the *dyak* or clerk of the church, and Oxana's father. By ill luck they all choose this Christmas Eve to call on her, and she has to hide them one at a time in empty sacks. Vakula, coming home, carries out the sacks and, finding that chance has thus put the Devil in his power, demands to be taken at once to St. Petersburg. The Devil obeys. Vakula is admitted to the Palace and graciously received by the great Catherine, who, being in an amiable mood, laughingly grants his request for a pair of her shoes, and the smith returns in triumph to Oxana, who is already regretting the supposed loss of her lover.

When a man takes up at fifty a subject so very like one he has treated at thirty-four, comparison of the two works can hardly fail to be illuminating. Beethoven, during the corresponding period of his life, advanced from the "Eroïca" to the "Hammerklavier" and the "Missa Solennis," Wagner from "Lohengrin" to "Tristan" and "Die Meistersinger." Before "May Night" Rimsky-Korsakov had written only one opera, "Pskovityanka." It is true that only two others, "Snegurochka" and "Mlada," intervened between the two Gogol works, but when he wrote "Christmas Eve" the composer had definitely adopted the theatre as his principal sphere of activity. During the first twenty-five years of his career, from 1865 to 1890, he had written only three operas; during the remaining eighteen years of his life he produced twelve. Moreover, the great orchestral works by which Rimsky-Korsakov is best known, the "Capriccio Espagnol," "Scheherazade," the "Easter Festival" Overture and the Piano Concerto, were all written in the period between "May Night" and "Christmas Eve."

But a mere glance at the two scores is all that is needed to see that Korsakov's style underwent no change at all comparable with Beethoven's or Wagner's. The work of 1894 does not differ materially from that of 1878, either in musical texture or in dramatic treatment. Like most of Rimsky-Korsakov's operas, they accept all the familiar conventions of classical Russian opera; melodic recitative, changing from declamation to definite tunes almost from bar to bar; occasional self-contained numbers, not always very deftly patched into the general fabric; nearly equal division of the interest between voices and orchestra, but with the voices slightly predominating; and so on. But it is obvious that considerable variation of treatment is possible within the limits of this convention. The lyrical element, for instance, with the self-contained "set numbers," may be emphasised, or it may be reduced to a minimum. Borodin definitely inclined to one tendency, Mussorgsky to the other. But Rimsky-Korsakov's practice varied considerably, according to the nature of the subject and to his own experimental inclination at the moment. The fact that the naïvely melodic element is much less important in "Christmas Eve" than in "May Night" is probably due to both causes.

The earlier work is, before everything else, lyrical. A much larger proportion of the score consists of musically independent numbers than does that of "Christmas Eve." The flow of melody is almost uninterrupted, for when the voices declaim the orchestra often picks up the threads. The melody may not always be of the highest value, but it is always undeniably alive. It helps along the most prosaic dialogue (e.g., the trio that opens the second act), provides a lovely background (the Pentecostal song in the first act), or adds an impudent commentary (as in the case of the piccolo solo, accompanied only by a side-drum roll, which makes merry over the village dignitaries as they threaten vengeance on the miscreants who have been playing tricks on them), as well as expressing the emotional content of the love scenes—the weakest parts of the score, as is so often the case in Russian operas—or hinting at the glamour of a summer night in the Ukraine, which Gogol paints so lovingly in his story. It seldom attempts to say very much, but

RIMSKY-KORSAKOV

its jolly, unaffected simplicity perfectly matches the subject. Only in the expressive passages where the composer is compelled to cut adrift from the folk-song idiom, fundamentally expressionless in Russia as in most countries, does the melodic inspiration lapse into the really commonplace.* But even when a dramatic situation seems inevitably to demand expressive music, the composer's flair for the picturesque and fantastic often offers him an avenue of escape. The opening of Act III, for instance, where Levko appears in the moonlight by the lake-side, is painted with all the orchestral skill one expects of Rimsky-Korsakov, but the music is more effective in a decorative than in an expressive capacity. The expression of Levko's feelings, intoxicated as he is with the beauty of the night, is beyond the composer's powers—as he soon proves by attempting it. But the situation is retrieved by

* The genuine folk-song element in both works is quite considerable. Rimsky-Korsakov borrowed most of his Malo-Russian tunes from A. I. Rubetz's collection of "216 Ukrainian Folk-Songs," and the score of "May Night" contains seven, that of "Christmas Eve" eight, melodies from this source. Thus Levko's first song, the trio and comic march in Act II, several of the choruses and various phrases in the part of the *golova's* sister-in-law in "May Night"—and the "kolyadki," Panas's comic song, Oxana's lament, Chub's duet with Solokha and other bits of melody in "Christmas Eve"—are all taken from this collection of Rubetz's.

the Cossack's naïve song with *pandura* accompaniment and after that, with the appearance of the russalkas, Rimsky-Korsakov is in his element; the scene which follows is perhaps the best part of the whole work. The *khorovod** of the russalkas suggests, particularly in the *poco più animato* sections:—

Ex. 40.

the *khorovod* ("Ronde des Princesses") in "The Fire Bird":—

Ex. 41.

* This chorus was based on sketches made for the St. John's Eve chorus of girls in Act II of "Mlada"—the collaborative "Mlada" of 1872, of course. When Rimsky-Korsakov returned to the abandoned libretto in 1890 and set the whole of it himself, he privately expressed his regret that he had not preserved the music of this chorus for its original purpose.

Not that there is a very close resemblance as regards the actual notes (though Stravinsky's counterpoint, creeping in drowsy semitones, is also foreshadowed in a later variation of Rimsky-Korsakov's melody), but it is interesting to see how thoroughly the roots of the early Stravinsky had struck into the soil of the preceding generation—just as a descending whole-tone scale for trombones in "May Night" itself, a few bars before the piccolo solo already mentioned, in turn calls up a memory of Glinka's "Ruslan."

"May Night," like "Pskovityanka" but unlike the majority of Rimsky-Korsakov's operas, has a full-length overture based on material used later in the work: some of the russalka music of the third act, Levko's song from the same act, part of the love-duet in Act I, and the finale of the opera. "Christmas Eve," on the other hand, has only a short introduction, "Holy Eve," leading without a break into the first act of the opera. This introduction repays study, however, for a great deal can be learned from it concerning the direction taken by Rimsky-Korsakov's musical thought. After half-a-dozen bars of common chords in a most uncommon progression (on descending thirds—E,

C sharp, A, F sharp, D, B, G—an obviously artificial arrangement of which Rimsky-Korsakov was remarkably fond) we get :—

Ex. 42.

Nothing could be less adventurous harmonically. The horn solo differs only by a single note from one in the russalka scene of "May Night."* The wavy triplet figure had always been one of the composer's favourite accompaniment devices; he uses it as the

* The fact that in Ex. 42 it is clearly a "telescoped" version of bars 6-8 throws an interesting light on Korsakov's tendency to slip into certain melodic grooves.

background to a horn solo in the "May Night" Overture, to go no further afield. In short, there is nothing in the musical substance which distinguishes it from a dozen passages in the earlier work. The difference lies in what one can only call the essence of the music. It is not merely that the "decorative" function of the music is here the only one. Not only genuine lyrical feeling has disappeared but every trace of natural musical fertility with it. No one can deny the originality of such music or its piquancy to the ear, but it is essentially lifeless. As Sir Henry Hadow has put it, "the composer must be the parent of his ideas, not their fabricator," and music like Ex. 42 (and more than one other theme in "Christmas Eve") is unquestionably *made*. It could only have been made by an imaginative mind, it is true, but the imagination brought into play here is not essentially creative; the composer is simply playing with sounds. It is evident that Rimsky-Korsakov's delight in music was always rather naïvely sensuous, a love of sound for sound's sake; at first a love of tunes, with a consequent pleasure in setting them off to the best advantage, later (as in this case) an almost childish delight in the striking juxtaposition of chords and timbres and in such colour-effects as rushing chromatic scale backgrounds on solo wind—frequently used in "Christmas Eve," as in the great orchestral works of a year or two earlier, but from which the score of "May Night" is quite free. The early orchestral "Sadko" and "Antar" may be adduced as evidence that piquant artificiality played a part in Rimsky-Korsakov's music from the first, but it was not until much later that he began to devise melodic formulæ like that in bars 5-8 of Ex. 42, which (of course divested of the trills) is used as a vocal melody in the first act. Here already is foreshadowed the Astrologer's music in the introduction to "The Golden Cockerel," thirteen years later still :—

Ex. 43.

a piece of mere cold-blooded ingenuity.

The lyrical element is still important in "Christmas Eve," however. The second tableau of Act I opens with a long aria, sung by Oxana as she admires herself in a mirror, full of arabesques and vocal cadenzas echoing clarinet cadenzas in Korsakov's familiar manner, which could be given without the least alteration as a concert number. But Vakula does his love-making to music even more characterless than Levko's in "A May Night":—

Ex. 44.

("*Thou* art both mother and father to me. Thou art dearest of all"; Oxana has been taunting him that his mother is a witch.) It is this falling off in the quality, even more than in the quantity, of the melodic element in "Christmas Eve" which is so significant. The fantastic nature of the story is often better matched with fragmentary motives and pungent chords, set off with frostily glittering orchestration, than with straightforward tunes. The disquieting point is the undistinguished character of the tunes when they do appear. This is particularly noticeable in the ballet music of Act III, the "games and dances of the stars" which occur as an interlude in Vakula's wild ride through the air. The ride itself is painted with Korsakov's usual orchestral skill, though the material on which the skill is exercised—rhythmic figures after the manner of Berlioz's "Ride to the Abyss"*—is hardly interesting enough to bear such extended treatment. As Vakula nears the Palace, a fanfare in polonaise rhythm is woven into the music, and the scene in the Palace itself is accompanied almost throughout by a brilliant polonaise of the conventional kind so often written by Russian composers.

Moreover, while in "May Night" the melodic invention is fresh and original, apart from the folk-song borrowings, in "Christmas Eve," as in all the later works, we find the composer weakly echoing himself in the most obvious way. Thus the second phrase of Oxana's first song, the mirror aria already mentioned:—

---

* It is curious that two or three years before the composition of "Christmas Eve," Rimsky-Korsakov had told Yastrebtsev that he did not consider the "Course à l'abîme" "real music, but rather an extraordinarily brilliant musical *decoration*." I was amused to find that the composer had applied to Berlioz's music the very word which I, not knowing this, had used to define the nature of his own.

Ex. 45.

is simply the opening of Snegurochka's first song :—

Ex. 46.

in slow *tempo* ! On the other hand, there are numbers in "Christmas Eve"—the "kolyada" choruses,* the humorous duet for Chub and Solokha in Act II, the second *(allegro)* part of the mirror aria, Oxana's lament in the last scene, the epilogue "in memory of Gogol" (most of them directly based on actual folk-melody, it will be noticed)—as fresh and delightful as anything in "May Night" and

* A custom very similar to our own carolling, but limited to Christmas Eve. The songs were usually about the birth of Christ, and at the end the singers, young men and girls of the village, would offer good wishes to the members of the household and receive presents of bread, money, etc. Gogol suggests that the word "kolyada" may be derived from an old Slavonic deity, one of the protectors of the sun-god in his battle with the powers of winter. Fanciful etymologists have found its origin in the Latin *kalendæ*. But Rimsky-Korsakov shared Gogol's opinion, for he makes Vakula, during his return from Petersburg, see the aerial procession of the Light Gods, Ovsenya and Kolyada, while the Christmas bells ring out from the village below.

which, as far as the musical texture is concerned, might belong to that score. (It would be difficult to find any pages in "Tristan" that might be transferred to "Lohengrin"!) Indeed, considered as a whole, "Christmas Eve" is perhaps the finer work of the two. If so much the less inspiration went to its making, the making itself is more skilfully done. When he wrote "May Night" Rimsky-Korsakov was wealthier, but by the time he reached "Christmas Eve" he had learned how to get better value for his money.

In "May Night" the themes have their immediate, superficial value only. Leit-motives are used but they could hardly be used less. Some of the music of the russalka scene is heard in the first act when Levko tells his sweetheart the story of the haunted house. (It is curious that in all Rimsky-Korsakov's operas, especially the later ones, the music associated with fantastic and supernatural scenes and characters is not only more highly seasoned harmonically, but more elaborately organised thematically, than that associated with the real and natural elements.) The old headman is associated throughout with two fragments of melody, often combined contrapuntally, to which he relates his never-ending reminiscence of the time when he was chosen as guide to the Empress Catherine; and another, related to one of these, which reminds us of his wooing of Hanna. In the last scene when the scribe examines the mysterious note, and once or twice later, a horn dreamily recalls the queen of the russalkas. That is all. The leit-motif is not used systematically or, except in the last mentioned instance, with dramatic value or subtlety.

In "Christmas Eve," on the other hand, there are a number of themes definitely associated throughout with Chub, with the Devil, with the stars, with the idea of flight, with witches, and so on. The theme of Vakula himself :—

Ex. 47.

is used with merciless consistency every time he appears, and with little modification or development (though perhaps the second bar of Ex. 44 is derived from it). And in addition to motives proper, there is a good deal of reminiscence of whole passages, a device which has a certain dramatic value—and a still greater, perhaps, in knitting together the whole musical fabric. Towards the end, for instance, when Vakula has brought back the shoes, his love-theme (Ex. 44) steals back on the clarinet* and the smith himself sings the same melody to which Oxana had previously taunted him.

One can even detect a difference in the nature of the humour in which both scores abound. In "May Night" the humour is more natural, a spontaneous bubbling over of high spirits. Unlike so many attempts at musical humour the music is genuinely funny. It would be difficult to listen to the *hopak* or the recitatives of the drunken Kalennik, to the *golova's* absurd wooing or to the ensembles in the second act without smiling, even at a concert performance in a language one did not understand. (Incidentally, the "laughter" in this act is a naturalistic record of the infectious, musical laugh of one of the composer's acquaintances.) Even the whole-tone scale already referred to, underlining the enraged headman's threats of punishment, has an irresistibly comic effect. But in "Christmas Eve" the humour is at once more subtle, more sophisticated and more laboured. The fact that the church

* A favourite dramatic device of Rimsky-Korsakov's. He uses it most effectively in "The Tsar's Bride."

clerk sings old liturgical melodies when he is making love to Solokha ought to be funny, Korsakov seems to have felt; but, actually, it is merely ridiculous. And the music which accompanies the absurd scene in Patsyuk's hut is bizarre and fantastic rather than humorous. Only the duet of the two old women in the last scene really recaptures the broad, frank humour of the earlier opera. In his later works, Rimsky-Korsakov's humour tends to take the form of grave and matter-of-fact musical treatment of absurdities, though in "The Golden Cockerel" it is both more obvious and more biting, humorous caricature flavoured with rather sophisticated wit, and in "Tsar Saltan" is tinctured with the delightful, indefinable something which gives that rambling opera its peculiar charm.

Rimsky-Korsakov's gradual transition from a simple, lyrical musical idiom to one in which artificiality, piquancy and technical sophistication predominated may be attributed to one or more of various causes, but it certainly has nothing in common with the normal process of development undergone by creative artists in general. It may have been due to mere pedantic absorption in musical ingenuities as his mastery of technique became more and more sure; to conscious modification conditioned by extra-musical factors, such as the problems of music-drama as an art-form; to actual exhaustion of natural melodic fertility; or to the possibility which cannot be entirely ruled out, that Rimsky-Korsakov never was fertile in the true sense and that his apparent melodic gift was purely imitative. There is evidence in favour of all these views, except the last. And in considering the modification of Rimsky-Korsakov's operatic, apart from that in his musical style, it is well to bear in mind that "Pskovityanka," his first stage-work, is a very self-conscious essay in the problems of musical drama as they presented themselves to the Russian composers of that period. Perhaps as he went on, his intellect and his instinct gave different answers to the same problems. We must remember that Korsakov was always painfully aware of his processes, even musically. No composer more *musically* introspective has ever lived, though he knew the artistic dangers of self-consciousness—"Self-analysis is fatal to creation."

It may be thought that, in comparing these two Gogol operas, I have laid too much emphasis on differences which are astonishingly small, considering the interval which separated them. But the very absence of any more obvious modification of style during fourteen years might surely be taken as evidence that the composer was lacking in the exuberance natural to the creative artist. And it is certainly true that the traces of sterility discernible in "Christmas Eve" are much more apparent in later works. Nor was Korsakov happily unaware of all this; on the contrary it is characteristic that he was far more acutely conscious of it than most of those about him were. Yastrebtsev, who saw a great deal of him during the composition of "Christmas Eve," tells us of his frequent moods of melancholy dissatisfaction and disillusionment. Even when the first two scenes were already finished, Korsakov spoke of the possibility of his not going on with the opera, as it was "not worth while." "You know," he added, "I see clearly that this music is far from being as good as that of 'Snegurochka,' for example, and that my talent is on the wane. And yet I don't find it *difficult* to write." We know from his memoirs that he had just been passing through one of those mental crisis which seem to afflict so many Russian artists in middle age. But how far this crisis was responsible for his despondency or partial sterility or both—or vice versa—it is impossible to do more than guess. They were almost certainly inter-related to some extent, but it would be only too easy to exaggerate the importance of this crisis by overlooking the fatal attractions which experiment and technical dexterity always held for the composer.

X.—"*SNOW MAIDEN.*"

THE gradual hardening and over-intellectualisation of Rimsky-Korsakov's musical tissue did not begin immediately after the composition of "May Night," for his melodic fertility is heard at its freshest in the opera which followed it, "Snegurochka" ("Snow Maiden"). The composer already begins, in the music associated with Tsar Berendey, to toy with finely wrought artificial thematic subtleties, to play that jig-saw game with fragmentary motives of which his later "miniature style" consists. But as a whole the music of "Snegurochka" sounds captivatingly spontaneous, so fresh and delightful that a good case might be made for placing it at the head of all Rimsky-Korsakov's operas. Musically it is in every way finer than "May Night." The composer was now completely master of his craft and completely *himself*. And he was conscious of it. "When I finished 'Snegurochka' I felt that I was a mature musician and that, as an opera-composer, I had firm ground under my feet." Leit-motives are already used far more liberally than in the two earlier operas, though not on Wagnerian lines, for Rimsky-Korsakov as yet knew his Wagner only very superficially. But apart from this material binding together of the music, "Snegurochka" has that unity of spirit which belongs only to living works of art. The transparence of its harmonic and orchestral texture, the flavour of its melodies, are unmistakable. It may not be literally true to say that music from any of Rimsky-Korsakov's other works would at once sound out of place if incorporated in this "spring fairy tale," but "Snegurochka" is such a living, clearly coloured whole, a musical world of its own, that it seems as if any such interpolation would be jarringly noticeable.

When Rimsky-Korsakov first came across Ostrovsky's dramatic poem in 1874* he was not impressed

* It had been produced in Moscow the year before, with incidental music (nineteen numbers) by Tchaïkovsky. When Rimsky-Korsakov's opera was brought out in January, 1882, Tchaïkovsky, far away in Rome, wrote to his publisher, Jurgenson, in terms which show how well-grounded was Rimsky-Korsakov's fear of giving offence to the other by following him in setting Gogol's "Christmas Eve": "Is it not equally unpleasant to you to feel that 'our subject' has been taken from us, and that Lel will now sing new music to the old words? It is as though someone had

by it, a fact which he explained to himself in after years by the reflection that he was then still too much under the influence of Mussorgsky's ideas about "naturalism" to be attracted by such an altogether unreal subject. But we must remember that in 1874 he had not yet begun to interest himself in the old Slavonic sun-worship which is the philosophical essence of "Snegurochka." It was not till a year or two later that in making his collection of folk-songs, the necessity of finding out something about the rites with which many of the songs were originally connected drove him to the study of authorities like Afanasev and Sakharov and aroused in him such an extraordinary interest in Slavonic mythology that "pictures of the old pagan time and its spirit rose before my inward eye with the greatest clearness and attracted me with irresistible power." From that time onward Rimsky-Korsakov tried to graft mythological elements on to nearly everything he touched, whether congruously or not. "May Night" had offered him very little scope. Beyond

---

forcibly torn away a piece of myself and offered it to the public in a new and brilliant setting. I could cry with mortification." But Tchaïkovsky afterwards had the grace to recognise the superiority of his rival's music. In 1887 he notes in his diary that he has "read through Korsakov's 'Snegurochka,' and was astonished at his mastery. I envy him and ought to be ashamed of it."

turning Gogol's "souls of the drowned" into russalkas and introducing quasi-ritualistic choruses and dances, there was nothing much to be done with it. So when in the February of 1880 he again read Ostrovsky's "Snegurochka," it was probably not so much the "marvellous poetic beauties" to which his eyes were now opened, as he thought, as the absolutely congenial nature of the fantastic-mythological subject which excited in him the wish to make an opera of it. In 1874 it had meant nothing to him; now it answered to all his inmost needs as an artist. And consequently it seemed to him that "there was no finer material in the world for me than this: there were no more poetic figures in existence than Snegurochka, Lel or the Spring Fairy, no better land than that of the Berendeys with its wonderful Tsar; there was no religion or philosophy more satisfying than the worship of the sun-god, Yarilo."

And to understand Rimsky-Korsakov properly we must realise that when he speaks like this he is not merely using ordinary enthusiastic hyperbole. He literally means what he says. He longed for absurd, delightful fairy-tale countries like the prehistoric land of the Berendeys, with its kindly despot and its gaily painted houses of carved wood, as Brahms longed for his lost childhood, Franck for heaven and Wagner for a new earth. In this intellectual rationalist, with his utter disbelief in "everything supernatural, fantastic or visionary," the instinctive longing for the irrational was sometimes so intense that he could not only as an artist create Nietzsche's "veil of illusion" but believe in it himself for the time being. The subject of "Snegurochka" awoke in him the dormant pantheist. Always an ardent nature-lover, his "sun worship" was a real and intense aspiration, strikingly like that which Richard Jefferies describes in "The Story of my Heart."*

Rimsky-Korsakov tells us in his memoirs how he wrote "Snegurochka" in the hot and thundery summer of 1880, at Stelëvo in the heart of the country, composing all day and every day—when he was not looking for mushrooms or helping his wife preserve fruit from the great garden, shaded with fruit-trees and "filled with the ceaseless twittering of birds." "In every gnarled branch or tree-trunk I saw the Wood Spirit or his dwelling; in the forest of Vol-

---

* "The Story of my Heart" was published in 1883, the year after the first performance of "Snegurochka." It is curious that two such different manifestations of the same primitive impulse in man should have appeared almost simultaneously.

chinets, the magic wood in which Mizgir lost himself; in an isolated hill, Mount Kopïtets, Yarilo's mountain." Publicly, in the "Record of my Life," Rimsky-Korsakov made only this fanciful confession. But the completeness and reality of his abandonment to illùsion is shown by his confession to Yastrebtsev that in old trees, the stream, Lake Vrevo, he saw something strange and supernatural. It seemed to him that the animals and birds, trees and flowers, were more conscious than men of the magical and supernatural, that they better understood the language of nature. "You will say that all this was dreadfully nonsensical, and yet it seemed to me that it was so in reality. I believed in it all as ardently as a child, as a dreamer who entirely gives himself up to his dreams, and yet—remarkably enough—the world seemed to me loftier, more comprehensible, and I was, as it were, fused with it."

So powerfully stirred, Rimsky-Korsakov found that the music poured from him easily. Directly he re-read the play, even before he rushed off to Moscow to get Ostrovsky's permission to take liberties with the libretto, ideas came thick and fast—"motives, themes and chord-progressions, while the moods and colours of particular moments became ever more distinct." During the summer at Stelëvo his thoughts flowed so quickly that he was unable to write "Snegurochka" directly in full score, as he had done "May Night," but was obliged to follow the more usual practice and make a piano score. The whole opera was completely sketched out in this way between June 1 and August 12. The scoring, for large orchestra, was done during the following winter, and a year later "Snegurochka" was given for the first time at the Maryinsky Theatre, Petersburg.

It is evident from all this, though the evidence of the music itself is sufficient, that "Snegurochka" was genuinely inspired. Yet it is curious to find how much even of this, probably the most spontaneous of all Rimsky-Korsakov's scores, was borrowed or calculated. The synthetic, rather than spontaneous, nature of the folk-songish melodies with which the score is strewn has already been referred to. In addition there are numerous borrowings of actual folk-songs: e.g., the second part of the choral ballet of the birds; three melodies in the "Butterweek" music of the Prologue appear as Nos. 41, 46 and 47 in Rimsky-Korsakov's own collection, Op. 24, and a fourth, to use the composer's own expression, "sacrilegiously reminds one of a melody in the Russian requiem mass"—here, he considered, restored to something like its original pagan form; the betrothal rites in the first act are introduced by a snatch of a song in praise of bachelorhood (Op. 24, No. 100) played by the clarinet, and the principal melody is a bridal song (Op. 24, No. 78); the opening of the third act, the festival in the Holy Wood—introduction, chorus and Bobïl's song about the beaver—is entirely based on folk-melodies (Op. 24, Nos. 16 and 54, and a dance-theme, a variant of the familiar "Kamarinskaya"); the millet sowing ritual and the antiphonal song to "Grandfather" Lado, the god of Spring and Love, which open "May Night" are repeated in the last act of "Snegurochka," while the people are waiting for the sunrise, but in this case Rimsky-Korsakov has used the two melodies to these words noted by Balakirev.* And then, in addition to lesser borrowings such as the pastoral motives for horn, clarinet and *cor anglais*, associ-

* From the Nizhny-Novgorod and Pskov Governments. They appear as Nos. 8 and 9 in Balakirev's "Collection of Forty Russian Folk-Songs." In "May Night" Rimsky-Korsakov kept more closely to a variant from the Saratov Government (No. 48 of his Op. 24.)

ated with the shepherd Lel, there is the call of the heralds in Act II when they summon the people to hear the Tsar's judgment, which the composer remembered from his childhood days when each summer a messenger would come from the Tikhvin Monastery, and to this melody, so like those of the old *bïliny*, summon the women of the village to help the monks with their hay-making. Yet all these borrowings sound so natural, fall so fittingly into place, that one accepts them without a murmur. It is the same with the bird-calls, "phonographically" reproduced in Beethoven's manner, not stylised and idealised in Wagner's—the cock-crow of the oboe at the very beginning (as it were, Nature's trumpet call heralding the coming of Spring), the cries of magpie, cuckoo, bullfinch and the rest. Rimsky-Korsakov's musical fantasy takes complete charge of this "given" material, weaving it into such delightful patterns, harmonising it with such freshness and clarity, tinting it with such bright, transparent orchestral colours, that it becomes as definitely *his* as if it had all sprung originally from his own brain. Rimsky-Korsakov wrote nothing more deliciously absurd, more perfectly characteristic, than the choral ballet of the birds in the Prologue, with its naïve piping tunes and that "ceaseless twittering" accompaniment straight from the garden at Stelëvo. Incidentally, another "twittering" theme, which appears first in the introduction :—

Ex. 48.

and later (in slower *tempo* on a solo horn) becomes one of the motives of the Spring Fairy, foreshadows a very important motif in "Kitezh." Rimsky-Korsakov in a fragmentary analysis of "Snegurochka," written in 1905 and published posthumously, calls Ex. 48 the theme of "general bird-twittering," the chorus of Nature, while the similar theme in "Kitezh" is identified with Fevronya, the pure child of Nature, and is evolved from the music of the murmuring forest.

Rimsky-Korsakov's own melodic invention is never more delightful than in "Snegurochka." The songs of Lel the shepherd singer are particularly beautiful. Rimsky-Korsakov had a special genius for the unaccompanied or barely accompanied song; his melodic lines are often so complete in themselves that to harmonise them is only to write out what is already fully implied, though he does this only too frequently. Lel's first song is entirely without accompaniment. The third, that which follows the tumblers' dance in the festival in the Holy Wood, accompanied at first only by a drum-roll, is specially interesting as it is the occasion of one of the earliest appearances of a melodic pattern (a) which constantly recurs throughout Rimsky-Korsakov's later work :—

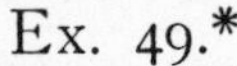
Ex. 49.*

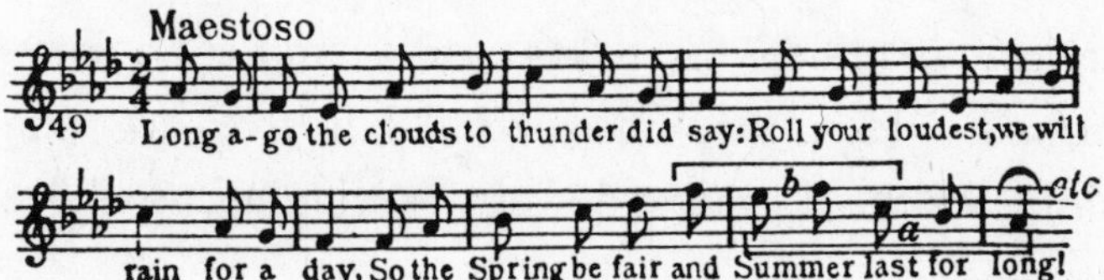

In this opera we find it also in the accompaniment to Snegurochka's first song (just after the words "I live for melody alone") and in the music of the kiss-scene in the third act. It appears again in "Sadko" (Nezhata's "Slava" at the end of the harbour scene), "The Tsar's Bride" (orchestral prelude to the sextet), "Tsar Saltan" (the Tsarevna Lebeda's

* I have followed Edward Agate's translation of the libretto throughout. (Bessel Edition: English agents, Boosey and Hawkes.)

song at the beginning of the last scene), "The Golden Cockerel" (Amelfa's music)—to mention only a few of the passages where it recurs in its original, unmodified form. Whence did Rimsky-Korsakov get it? Probably from the familiar "Sidel Vanya," the chief melody of the *andante cantabile* of Tchaïkovsky's D major Quartet, for it is not, like most of the other formulæ which recur in Rimsky-Korsakov's music, a pattern common to a number of folk-songs. In addition to these unchanged reappearances it frequently recurs in slightly modified forms, as, for example, in Fevronya's glorious phrase in "Kitezh" as she addresses the "strange flowers" springing up about her:—

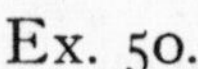

Ex. 50.

One expects, of course, to be able to trace the derivation of a great many of a composer's themes from a single germ. The curious point is that Rimsky-Korsakov, in these later operas, so often repeated formulæ with only the slightest modification or even with none at all. There is remarkably little evidence in Rimsky-Korsakov of the operation of that ripening, continually modifying and developing process one finds going on in the minds of other composers. His melodic thought slips easily into old, familiar channels without wearing them into fresh forms. But Ex. 49 (a) is too important to be dismissed as something accidentally remembered in after years. A little monograph might be written on the function of its first three notes alone in Rimsky-Korsakov's *melos*, and another on the group (b) in Ex. 49, an unconscious modification of Ex. 48.* It is no exaggeration to say that the last bar-and-a-half of Ex. 49 contains the essence of Rimsky-Korsakov's most characteristic melodic thought.

All this curious arrangement and rearrangement of (not development of, or growth from) a few elementary melodic patterns, rather suggesting the old Chinese game of tangrams, must of course have been quite unconscious. But Rimsky-Korsakov often plays quite consciously with tiny motives in the same way. He begins to do it here in the Tsar Berendey's music, in which we can watch his first

* Compare also Ex. 39 in "Pskovityanka."

experiments in this "miniature style." The Tsar's theme :—

Ex. 51.

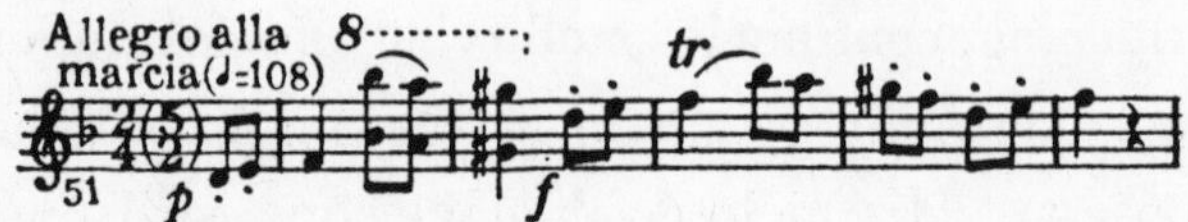

is dissected into its constituent three-note motives, which are rearranged :—

Ex. 52.

and the new figure thus obtained counterpointed with a previously heard march-theme (extended from the first four notes of Ex. 51) :—

Ex. 53.

all in the brief march which accompanies the entry of the Tsar and his courtiers in Act II. But there is still very little of this artificial mosaic-music in "Snegurochka." The fantastic element in the music is prominent only in the snowstorm of the Prologue and in the scene of the enchanted wood. Yet it is characteristic of Rimsky-Korsakov that he was particularly pleased with the chord, made up of the six notes of the whole-tone scale, which he devised for the moment when the Wood Spirit seizes Mizgir from behind.

But in one's memories of the opera these moments are lost amidst the mass of purely lyrical music : the Spring Fairy's aria in the Prologue, Snegurochka's arietta, "Ah ! what woe is mine !" and her charming "Gathering Berries" song (of which the beautiful *adagio* section, recollected in the third act when Snegurochka finds herself abandoned by Lel, is the forerunner of such masterpieces as Marfa's great aria in "The Tsar's Bride" and Fevronya's "praise of solitude" in "Kitezh"), Lel's songs, the Tsar's two cavatinas, the love music, the hymn to the Tsar, and the final chorus in 11/4 time in praise of Yarilo. The love-music is, as so often in Russian opera, a little insipid, just as the element of human tragedy in the story is quite unmatched in the music. But there is genuine warmth and passion in the orchestral passage which accompanies the "kiss scene" and in Snegurochka's ecstatic surrender to Mizgir in the last act, where part of her chief theme (which the composer intentionally made "bright, graceful and playful, but cold in spite of its liveliness") is transformed into a phrase which perfectly expresses the warm, human emotion she now feels for the first time. If this lyrical current in "Snegurochka" sometimes runs thin and degenerates into mere prettiness, as in the schoolgirls'-operetta-chorus of flowers at the beginning of the last act, it also broadens into passages of marvellous beauty, such as the scene of the blind *gusli*-players which opens Act II. To a few simple chords on piano and harp (a device borrowed from Glinka for the suggestion of these old national instruments), the curtain goes up revealing a hall in the Tsar's palace, fantastically carved and painted like all the houses of the Berendeys. The Tsar himself sits on a golden throne, painting on a pillar, while his blind singers, playing their *guslis*, sing his praises. Nothing could be simpler than the music, a modal melody sung by a few basses in unison (with a curious two-part refrain) and accompanied only by the quiet harp and piano chords :—

Ex. 54.

yet the scene is one of the most memorable in all Rimsky-Korsakov's operas. He often introduced similar episodes of bards and pilgrims singing to the accompaniment of national instruments in later works, but never again achieved anything quite as gravely beautiful. The modal nature of the melody (æolian) is characteristic of another tendency of Rimsky-Korsakov's, to which he allowed full play in "Snegurochka." He had already introduced modal folk-melodies in "May Night"; now for the first time he actually composed in the old modes. And he wrote in them easily and naturally, reopening (as he justly claimed) a rich old vein neglected by all but one or two Western composers—Liszt in his "Totentanz" (variations on the "Dies Iræ") for piano and orchestra, and in the middle section (on the "Pange lingua") of his "Night Procession" (Episode from Lenau's "Faust"), and Berlioz in his "Nubian Dance" and his overture to "The Flight into Egypt." Lel's first song and the hymn of the Berendeys before the trial in Act II are particularly happy examples of Korsakov's modal writing. The pentatonic scale is another tonal characteristic of many Russian folk-melodies (e.g., that which figures here as Bobïl's "beaver" song), which left its mark on Rimsky-Korsakov's music from the "Snegurochka" period onward. Some of his most typical melodies (for instance, that which opens and closes the Hindu merchant's song in "Sadko") are pentatonic. On the other hand, the curious clipped mezzo-recitative phrases of the dialogue between Kupava and the Tsar :—

Ex. 55.

the exact musical equivalent of the style and metre of Russian fairy-tale poetry, have no prototypes in popular music. This highly effective type of recitative was the composer's own invention, here introduced only episodically, but very freely employed in the later fairy-tale operas.

In "Snegurochka" and the coeval "Legend" ("Skazka") for orchestra, based on the prologue to Pushkin's "Ruslan and Lyudmila," Rimsky-Korsakov definitely emerged as a master orchestrator and a highly individual one. We cannot study the scoring of his early compositions, as he afterwards reorchestrated everything written before "May Night." We only know, from his own account, that from the beginning he had an instinctive feeling for orchestral colour and that even in the 'sixties he was looked upon as the best orchestrator of the "Kuchka." Perhaps his early scoring was effective enough in a rather crude way. As we have seen, his editorial work on the scores of Glinka's operas had left him deeply impressed with Glinka's delicate and transparent orchestral texture, and hence "May Night," the first of his scores which we can study in its original form, is possibly less individual than the earlier works. This period of Glinka-worship probably served to purify his orchestral style as, on his own confession, it did his harmonic and contrapuntal texture. But in "Snegurochka" the composer's inclination for bright, primary colours—and colour for colour's sake—asserted itself (probably we ought to say, reasserted itself). He has called attention himself to the profusion of solo passages for violin, 'cello, flute, oboe and cor anglais and horn, above all for the clarinet, which was at that time a pet instrument of his. And it is these bright, unmixed colours, the musical counterpart of the gaily painted houses of the Berendeys, which give the opera so much of its translucent quality and unique flavour. Rimsky-Korsakov never quite recaptured this delightful naïveté of timbre, for before he wrote his next opera, "Mlada," he had undergone an experience which left indelible marks on his later scores. The "Ring" had been given in St. Petersburg (1888) by a German company under Muck. Wagner's treatment of the orchestra "dumbfounded" him and in his memoirs he naïvely confesses how he and Glazunov attended all the rehearsals and industriously studied and copied the German master's methods. And this was the mature master who, the year before, had produced such marvels of orchestration as "Scheherazade," the "Capriccio Espagnol" and the "Easter" Overture! Humility is a virtue, no doubt, and in the long run Rimsky-Korsakov benefited from this fertilisation of his style by Wagner's. "Mlada" was the only work in which his orchestral writing was really saturated by Wagnerian methods; already in "Christmas Eve," still more in "Sadko," his individuality began to reassert itself, all the richer for the experience. But one cannot help regretting the fatal ease with which Rimsky-Korsakov succumbed to temporary fascinations.

So "Snegurochka," the first fruit of the mature Rimsky-Korsakov as purified by Glinka and still untainted by Wagner, was also the last in the sphere of opera. Important as the naïvely lyrical element remained in his work, it was never again almost the sole one. But it is interesting to see how far Rimsky-Korsakov had progressed in the use of leit-motives in "Snegurochka" while he was still acquainted with Wagner "only a little and very superficially." His claim that he employed them quite differently from Wagner seems to be largely justified. They do not supply the material from which the orchestral part is almost wholly woven; they are still used dramatically, to make points, rather than systematically. But already in "Snegurochka" Korsakov had advanced far beyond "May Night," and the hearing of the "Ring" confirmed his tendency to Wagnerian "logic" so that by the time he wrote "Christmas Eve," as we have seen, he had begun to organise his leit-motif system very thoroughly indeed. As he points out in his memoirs, his leit-motives are often fragments of extended melodies such as that of Snegurochka herself and the Tsar's theme, Ex. 51. The Tsar's first cavatina, for instance, is accompanied by the motif (a) in Ex. 52, treated as an *ostinato* figure on a solo 'cello. And then again Korsakov uses mere chord-progressions or even single unusual chords, like that of the Wood Spirit, "more difficult to distinguish than Wagner's leit-motives, which often remind one of coarse military trumpet-calls."He dwells on this point with characteristic self-satisfaction, oblivious of the uselessness in opera of making points which can only be appreciaated by "a good, trained ear." Rimsky-Korsakov often became so deeply engrossed in the purely intellectual aspects (one is often tempted to say, the mere "paper" aspect) of music, that he quite lost sight of the true function of devices like the leit-motif. He forgot that a curious chord is likely to interest even a trained musician more for its own than for the action's sake, that it communicates no feeling and evokes no memory —except of its own previous appearance.

In the already mentioned analysis of "Snegurochka," Rimsky-Korsakov distinguished between the true leit-motives in the work and those themes and complete melodies which recur, partly or as wholes, as reminiscences for the sake of dramatic effect. The same distinction may be applied to the motives of all his later operas. But in all of them there is a great deal of important material which does not recur at all, which serves its purpose episodically and is then thrown aside; Rimsky-Korsakov never went quite as far as Wagner in weaving his musical fabric entirely from leit-motives, except perhaps in the unimportant "Kashcheï the Immortal." Nor, curiously enough, are Rimsky-Korsakov's theme-reminiscences always dramatic in purpose; sometimes their function is purely formal. In "May Night" the composer had already broken away from "dramatic truth" enough to give symmetrical *musical* shape to separate numbers. Beginning with "Snegurochka" he now attempted to give a distinct, architectural pattern to bigger stretches of music (scenes like the "Butterweek" episode, that of the blind *gusli*-players and the games in the Holy Wood), a tendency which he pushed to its extreme limit in parts of "'Sadko" and "Kitezh." In accordance with the same desire to formalise, he also organised the key-schemes of his operas with as much care as if they had been symphonic works. "Snegurochka" and all the later operas were laid out in accordance with a carefully prepared modulation plan, a plan not arbitrary but conditioned by two factors, the composer's peculiarly acute sense of key-colour and this need for architectural cohesion and symmetry. Rimsky-Korsakov's feeling for the "absolute" quality and colour of each key had begun to awaken as early as 1867, but "Snegurochka" was the first composition in which it played a predominant part in determining the choice of keys for each part of the work. Thus the idea of Spring is connected throughout the opera with A major, "the key of youth, gladness, Spring and dawn," as he calls it in the "Record of my Musical Life." D flat is associated with warmth and love, as in the Spring Fairy's aria in the Prologue, the song in which Lel tells the Tsar that his gift of song comes from the Sun-God ("In my words and in my songs brightly burn his glowing rays"), the kiss scene, and the love-duet for Snegurochka and Mizgir. D major is the colour of bright daylight; A minor suggested to Rimsky-Korsakov "the glow of sunset reflected on a white, cold, snow-covered winter landscape"; and so on. Rimsky-Korsakov did not, of course, allow himself to be rigidly bound by these associations. There are plenty of passages in "Snegurochka" and the later operas where this rather tormenting obsession of his seems to have left him in peace. But it would be quite true to say that he associated certain keys with particular moods and emotions as consciously and consistently as he did leit-motives with characters.

"Snegurochka" must be given an important place in Rimsky-Korsakov's life-work for another, a non-musical, reason. "Pskovityanka" is pure, realistic drama. "May Night" is a humorous-fantastic tale told for its own sake, with mythological trimmings of no special significance. But with "Snegurochka" begins Rimsky-Korsakov's dabbling with that symbolism one discerns dimly in "Sadko," more clearly in "Kitezh," and which, turned bitter, gives "The Golden Cockerel" its subtle flavour of irony. Rimsky-Korsakov read into this "Spring fairy-tale" a deeper significance than Ostrovsky perhaps intended, possibly more than he himself had seen in it at first. Years afterwards when he sat down, in 1905, to analyse this favourite work, he divided its characters into three categories: the purely mythical incarnations of natural forces, like Snegurochka's parents Spring and Frost; the ordinary mortals, like Kupava and Mizgir; and the three half-real, half-mythical characters—Snegurochka herself, the wise old Tsar Berendey, and the shepherd singer Lel. And it was this last group that particularly interested him, especially Lel. The Tsar is the perfect "paternal" ruler. He personifies the social life of a legendary golden age when men were happier because they were closer to Nature, when kings were also priests and the gods still real and visible.* As Rimsky-Korsakov points out, the Tsar is "ever old" as Lel is "ever young." They represent things which are ageless and timeless. The significance of Snegurochka herself, Spring outside like her mother, Winter within like her father, is not so clearly defined. She seems to

* At the very end of the opera Yarilo is seen on the summit of his sacred hill—a youth robed in white, bearing in his hands a human head and a sheaf of corn.

be merely a figure in a pretty fairy-tale, one more of those fairy beings, common to folk-lore the world over, whose gratified longing for human things leads to their destruction. But Lel is highly significant. He is the ideal type of folk-artist, a forerunner of Sadko. Like Sadko, he personifies music itself and its miracle-working power. (And like Sadko, too, he is rather heartless and irresponsible.) He gets his music, his power, immediately from the sun, from nature, and it is difficult to avoid the conjecture that the composer saw something of himself in the legendary figures of Lel and Sadko. There is, however, no trace of subjective expression in Lel's music (or in Sadko's).

And there is no trace of meaning, and little of definite emotion, in the music of the opera as a whole. The composer's possible self-identification with Lel and the deeper meaning we know he read into the poem are not expressed musically, only observed with Korsakov's characteristic detachment. It is impossible to agree with Russian critics like Lapshin, who sees in this "pantheistic Hymn to Nature and glowing apotheosis of love" a "worthy companion-piece to 'Tristan'" and who draws a parallel between Snegurochka's final "And yet I faint! With ecstasy or pain?" and Isolde's "Liebestod"! Rimsky-Korsakov's music is never more than that of a delightful fairy-tale. But it is so charming and, in its way, so perfect that one can understand the composer's "conviction" (in 1892, with "Sadko" not yet written) "that 'Snegurochka' is my best work," even if one cannot endorse his amusing, and characteristically complacent, reflection that it was "not only that but perhaps, on the whole, the best of all contemporary operas."

XI.—"SADKO."

THE story of Sadko, the poor minstrel who became rich through the love of the Sea King's daughter, which occurs in the eleventh century "Novgorod cycle" of *bïliny* or epic legends, had attracted Rimsky-Korsakov as early as 1867, when he wrote a short symphonic poem on the subject.* The idea of turning it into an opera had occurred to him in the 1880's but nothing definite came of it till the summer of 1894, when the musicologist Findeisen sent him the outline of a libretto. Rimsky-Korsakov was not altogether satisfied with Findeisen's plan and finally decided again to be his own librettist, drawing on the story of "The King of the Sea," from Afanasev's "Russian Fairy Tales," the "Kniga Golubinaya" or "Dove Book," and other sources for his text and for various incidents not found in the original Sadko legend. Stassov had a hand in the planning of this as of so

* His Opus 5. It was revised in 1891.

many other Russian operas and it was on his suggestion that Rimsky-Korsakov inserted the first scene, that of the banquet in the council-room at Novgorod. The composer had already decided to utilise the material of his early symphonic poem again in the opera.

As usual Rimsky-Korsakov spent the summer of 1894 in the country, on the estate of Vechasha by the shores of Lake Pezno, "an enchanting spot of earth" of which he gives a delightful picture in his memoirs. He was working hard at "Christmas Eve," but he could not get "Sadko" out of his head and various ideas—the melody of Sadko's aria in the fifth scene and the first of the songs of the *gusli*-player, Nezhata, among others occurred to him at this period. He takes an almost Pepysian pleasure in recalling precisely where these thoughts visited him—"on the long bathing-stage built out into the lake. It led out through high thick rushes; on one side one saw the fine old willows of the garden, on the other stretched Lake Pezno."

The completion of "Christmas Eve" and the difficulties attending its production, with other matters, thrust "Sadko" into the background, and although Rimsky-Korsakov was full of ideas, and the libretto of the work as originally planned was practically finished, only the first scene was completed when the composer returned to Vechasha in 1895. This summer was entirely devoted to "Sadko." The first, second, fourth, fifth, sixth and seventh tableaux were written, and the first and second actually scored, when the composer made a curious addition to his plan by deciding to introduce Sadko's faithful wife, Lyubava, who was mentioned but did not appear in the original version. This interpolation, which necessitated the writing of the third tableau as we now have it, as well as additions to the fourth and seventh tableaux, seems to have been suggested by V. I. Belsky, a man of varied intellectual gifts—jurist, scientist and mathematician—who was afterwards to be the librettist of "Tsar Saltan," "Kitezh" and "The Golden Cockerel." Rimsky-Korsakov had met Belsky the previous winter in St. Petersburg and found in him not only the possessor of common interests in Russian antiquity and Russian folk-music, but also an enthusiastic admirer of his own compositions and those of the so-called "new Russian school" in general. Belsky was spending this summer on an estate only about six miles from Vechasha, and the two men passed much time together. Belsky suggested various additions to the plan of "Sadko," with the result that, as the composer afterwards admitted, the work became too long. At first Rimsky-Korsakov could not make up his mind to any alterations in his scheme. Not until the opera in its original form was practically finished did a curious circumstance turn the scale. The composer tells us that he felt a vague wish to write something in the key of F minor which he had long neglected and which did not appear in "Sadko." It was this "vague wish" which "irresistibly" impelled him to compose Lyubava's lament in that key. The aria satisfied him and he at once asked Belsky to write the text of the remainder of the third tableau. (The text of Lyubava's song is by Rimsky-Korsakov himself.) The completion of the work was thus delayed and Rimsky-Korsakov records how, towards the end of the winter, he was overcome by fatigue and disgust for work, a feeling he then experienced for the first time but which afterwards recurred regularly just before the completion of every big composition. He relates an incident which shows the extent of his mental fatigue. After finishing the scoring of the sixth tableau he was overcome with dismay at the thought of the labour which still lay before him, of orchestrating the last scene. It was only the finding of the score, as he was turning over his papers, that reminded him that this was already finished.

Rimsky-Korsakov considered that "Sadko" marked the end of the middle period of his career as an opera composer. It was a work of which he was particularly proud. He grouped it with "Mlada" and "Christmas Eve," speaking of these two operas as "large-scale studies for 'Sadko,'" and, though a candid and surprisingly objective critic of his own work, he dwelt with much satisfaction on many passages of "Sadko." The "Gold! Gold!" scene of the fourth tableau, indeed the whole of the harbour scene, pleased him especially, and he considered the lullaby which Volkhova sings to the sleeping Sadko at the beginning of the last tableau, and the music of her disappearance, the best pages of fantastic music he had written. Yet, strangely enough (though the composer does not remark on the fact), some of the music which he himself considered the best in this splendid mature work —Sadko's descent to the submarine kingdom, the general dance which concludes the wedding revels, and the prelude to the last tableau—is actually taken from the symphonic poem of 1867. And as regards this early orchestral piece, Rimsky-Korsakov many years afterwards not only admitted that his music was derivative, but frankly avowed the precise sources which fed his musical fantasy in writing it. The passage so marvellously painting the swell of the calm sea, the profound breathing of the infinite ocean desert, which opens and closes the poem (in the opera it serves as the prelude to the first scene and its theme permeates the whole work as a sea-motif) was harmonically modelled on Liszt's "Ce qu'on entend sur la montagne," and the storm was suggested by Liszt's "Mephisto Waltz" and Balakirev's not yet finished "Tamara." The music of the Sea King's festival "is harmonically, even perhaps melodically, a little reminiscent of my favourite among Balakirev's songs, 'The Goldfish,' and of the introduction to the 'Russalka's' recitative in Dargomïzhsky's opera of the same name." Sadko's descent was likewise a reminiscence of the carrying-off of Lyudmila in Glinka's "Ruslan," except that Glinka's descending whole-tone scale was replaced by another artificial scale, consisting of alternate tones and semitones. Rimsky-Korsakov became strangely enamoured of this scale, using it again in the third movement of "Antar" and in various later works. It plays a very important part in the operatic version of "Sadko," being employed, in both ascending and descending forms, either as a simple scale or as the basis of a chord-progression in the second tableau (in which the Sea Princess and her sisters first appear to Sadko), during the intermezzo between the fifth and sixth tableaux (Sadko's descent), in the submarine ballet, at the climax of the storm, at the point where the curtain rises on the last tableau and Sadko and the Princess are seen in the meadow by Lake Ilmen, and again in the accompaniment to the Princess's lullaby.

There are, naturally, few traces of Liszt in the operatic "Sadko," though Glinka and Balakirev so thoroughly permeated Rimsky-Korsakov's musical personality that one occasionally detects the shadow of one or the other in the background of even such a mature work as this. And there are occasional reminiscences of Wagner. Most of these coincidences of musical thought (they are no more), the swan-motif in the second tableau, the incessant violin-figure of the "Tannhäuser" overture in the accompaniment to the Venetian merchant's song, and the rest, are unimportant. But it is curious to notice how, on their first appearance, Volkhova's sisters are much more nearly related to the Rhine-maidens, or even to the nymphs of the Venusberg, than to Rimsky-Korsakov's own russalkas in his "May Night" of eighteen years earlier. When the Sea Princess's sisters come out of the water to Sadko in the second tableau, the music plainly announces that Sadko is Siegfried approaching his end and that Lake Ilmen has somehow become the Rhine :—

Ex. 56.*

But in fairness it must be admitted that, in spite of

* A passage which Rimsky-Korsakov seems to have recollected when he wrote the accompaniment to Gryaznoy's confession in "The Tsar's Bride."

these resemblances and of the fairly elaborate system of leit-motives, "Sadko" is in no sense a Wagnerian opera. It is not only Rimsky-Korsakov's best opera (in the sense that it contains much of his best music in each of his different styles and that the musical level is more consistently high throughout), but his most individual—that in which he is most completely and exuberantly himself and most profoundly Russian. He may have been exaggerating when he claimed that in "Sadko" he had written music "the true character of which could only be appreciated by an audience Russian to the core," but it is certainly true that "Sadko" is Russian in every fibre. Although a picture, not a searching analysis, it is a marvellous evocation of the spirit of a people. The spirit is idealised, no doubt; Novgorod never could have been like this fairy-tale city even in its prime, in the half-historical, half-legendary time of the old epic songs when Christianity began to mingle with the old pagan beliefs and for a time lived with them, side by side—never, as Rimsky-Korsakov believed, quite conquering them. The darker streaks in the national character are suppressed in "Sadko." Just as the hero's fortune is what the artist's fortune *should* always be, the

Russia of "Sadko" is an ideal Russia, the land of the Berendeys brought forward in time, made a little more real, commercialised—and not quite so well governed.

Something has already been said of the episodic, undramatic nature of Russian opera at its best, and "Sadko" is an outstanding example, comparable in this respect with "Boris" and "Prince Igor." In none of his earlier works, except perhaps "Mlada," had Rimsky-Korsakov quite so frankly thrust the dramatic element into the background. Even in "Mlada" there is drama in intention, only, as he admitted, "the description of old customs and the fantastic element come too prominently to the fore." But "Sadko" is deliberately styled "opera-*bïlina*"* and the composer carefully emphasises the fact that it is no drama, but a series of scenes from an epic put on the stage and set to music. The story is little more than a pretext for brilliant stage-pictures and for music—above all for music, which Rimsky-Korsakov had by this time begun to consider definitely the most important constituent of

* The *bïliny* are epic legends, popular in origin, dealing with Vladimir the Great and other half-legendary heroes, handed down orally (by singing) among the peasants for many generations.

opera. How far he had drifted from the dramatic realism of Dargomïzhsky, Mussorgsky and his own "Pskovityanka" (and how radically his views differed from Wagner's) may be seen from his prefatory notes to the score of "Sadko": "I am convinced that an opera libretto should be considered and judged only as an integral part of the music. Apart from the music it serves only as a filling-out of the bare action; it is certainly not an independent literary work. I have not hesitated to take liberties with the poetic metre wherever the music demanded them. In opera the poetic rhythm must be subordinated to the musical, not vice versa." So far had he travelled from "the note as the direct expression of the word"! And just as the poetic metre is made subservient to that of the music, the stage action is to a certain extent moulded to a musical form. Rimsky-Korsakov's tendency to purely musical architecture in the build of opera-scenes, noticeable as early as "Snegurochka," is brought to its highest development in the fourth tableau of "Sadko," the harbour scene with its ever-changing mass of people—merchants, pilgrims, buffoons, soothsayers and elders. When he speaks of "the clear and broadly laid out symphonic form (somewhat in the manner of a rondo)" of this scene, up to the point where the hero enters, the composer is using quite accurate terms—although we must accept with caution his use of the word "symphonic." Rimsky-Korsakov's symphonic construction was always sectional rather than organic (think of "Scheherazade," for instance), and his music is never symphonic in the sense that Wagner's is. It is symphonic in outline but not in growth and texture.

"Sadko" is, in a sense, an affair of superimposed planes, one background behind another. But the backgrounds are so brilliantly painted that perspective is destroyed and the significance of the individual figures in the foreground diminished to vanishing point. And yet this very defect, as it apparently is, deepens the work's charm, underlining its resemblance to some archaic tapestry come to life. Furthest in the background is the sea, its confused murmur painted in a musical pattern, half-realistic, half quaintly stylised, like the stiff waves in some archaic painting or on an old chart, yet fresh and full of savour. For a sailor-composer Rimsky-Korsakov was not prolific of seascapes (and he was quite content to use the "wave" motif of

"Scheherazade" again in "Tsar Saltan") but the sea prelude to "Sadko," written, as we must remember, soon after his long cruise in the "Almaz," is a study direct from the life. And the sea music does more than paint a mood. (In fact there can be no question of the prelude's preparing the hearer's mind as the prelude to "Rheingold" does, for the curtain does not go up on a sea scene.) The sea is the ground-tone of the whole opera, and its motif recurs like a motto-theme throughout the work, being thundered out in a triumphant *fortissimo* at the very end.

When the curtain rises on the first tableau,* the hall of the feasting merchants, we come to the second background—the people of Novgorod. For the first time since "Pskovityanka," Rimsky-Korsakov now makes the chorus (and individuals, like Nezhata, who are representative types rather than characters) a chief protagonist. There are finely constructed crowd-scenes of popular life in most of Rimsky-Korsakov's operas; in fact, the harbour

* The seven tableaux of the opera may be divided into three or five acts. In the first case tableaux one and two constitute the first act; three and four, the second; and five, six and seven, the third. Or the first, fourth and seventh tableaux may be treated as separate acts, the second and third, and fifth and sixth, tableaux being grouped together.

scene in "Sadko" is essentially only an elaboration of the market-scene which opens the second act of "Mlada"; but in none of his other operas has the chorus anything like such a predominant rôle throughout the work. It is true the people are only superficially and idealistically painted, even in the kaleidoscopically brilliant fourth tableau, not studied in Mussorgsky's manner. Yet their rôle is no less important in "Sadko" than in "Boris."

In the first scene two very different types are sharply contrasted—the proud, boastful merchants and the buffoons who have to amuse them, the two extremities of the social scale. Each is characterised by folkish music, the dance-tunes of the buffoons being specially typical of Rimsky-Korsakov's essays in this genre, and at the end of the scene the merchants' chorus is combined with the dance music. All this provides the most important element of the scene, though the relatively unimportant solo parts of Nezhata and Sadko himself are more interesting to the student of Rimsky-Korsakov's music. The song of Nezhata, the young gusli-player (the part is written for a contralto), which comes as an interlude between the over-long opening chorus and the striking chorus in 11/4 time (all for male voices only), introduces the element of the old epic legends, in the atmosphere of which "Sadko" is steeped from beginning to end. He sings the *bïlina* of the Kiev hero, Volkh Vseslavich, to a monotonous sing-song, half melody, half recitative, of the kind to which these old tales were sung or recited by many generations of Russian peasant bards. Some of these *bïlina* melodies, taken down by Mussorgsky from the singing of Ryabinin, one of the last of these bards, are given by Rimsky-Korsakov in his "Hundred Russian Folk-Songs," and the melody of one of them, the song of Volga and Mikula, is sung by the two monks in the last scene of "Boris." But in "Sadko" Rimsky-Korsakov uses the style of this peculiar *bïlina*-recitative very extensively. It is this—"drawn," as the composer puts it, "like a scarlet thread through the whole opera"—which does so much to give "Sadko" its unique flavour. Sadko's own recitatives, all in this style, are specially noteworthy; for instance, the phrase :—

Ex. 57.

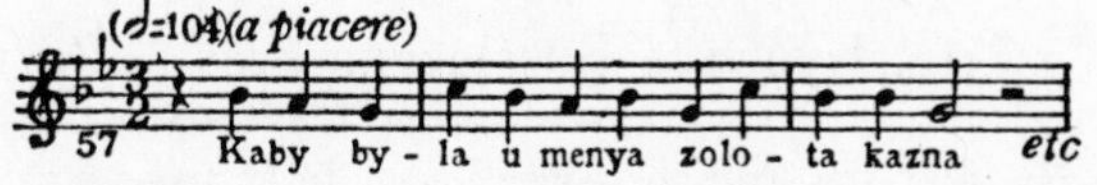
(♩=104)(a piacere)
57
Kaby by - la u menya zolo - ta kazna etc

to which he begins to tell the Novgorod merchants

what he would do if he were as rich in gold as they, a phrase which, in one form or another, assumes almost the importance of a leit-motif in the course of the work. The incessantly repeated phrase of the blind pilgrims in the fourth tableau :—

Ex. 58.

Andante
58
Ne dva zverya to so bi - ralisya, Ne dva liutye sokho-dilisya,
etc.

is not imitated, but a genuine fragment of *bïlina* song to which the legend of the holy "Dove Book" was recited.* The falling third cadences of both Ex. 57 and Ex. 58 are specially characteristic. Such melodic patterns woven again and again into the score subtly impregnate it with their archaic flavour.

All the real scenes of "Sadko," which are as usual differentiated from the fantastic ones by their harmonic simplicity and the diatonic nature of their melodies, are similarly dominated by the chorus and have the same epic character—with one exception. The third tableau, much of it a monologue for Sadko's wife, Lyubava Busslaevna, was not a very

* See No. 4 of the Filippov collection of forty folk-songs, harmonised by Rimsky-Korsakov. Another song connected with the "Golubinaya Kniga" is given in his Op. 24.

happy afterthought. The "F minor aria" itself is no masterpiece and the whole scene, with the later episodes in which Lyubava makes her appearance, seems to belong to the world of "The Tsar's Bride" rather than that of "Sadko." Those of its phrases which have the authentic ring of Rimsky-Korsakov at his best are all more or less exact reminiscences. The emphatic cadence of the unison orchestral passage which opens the scene is directly taken from Lel's first song in "Snegurochka." And Lyubava's joyous phrase, "Here he comes, my husband, my darling":—

Ex. 59.

(♩=132) Allegro
59
To i - det, to i - det muzhe-nek, mil na-de - zha moï!

is simply a (clearly unconscious) rearrangement of the melodic elements in the song which in the preceding scene Sadko has sung for Volkhova's sisters to dance to ("Sound, sound, my gusli," etc., Ex. 60). The patterns of 49 (a) and (b) provide the substance of both tunes,* yet Ex. 59 seems to be an immediate recollection of Ex. 60, without there being any dramatic or other reason to lead one to suppose that the

* The trumpet-theme which serves as a "Novgorod"-motif is also based on Ex. 49 (b), or rather on the form Ex. 48.

Ex. 60.

composer made it so consciously and intentionally. And it is equally doubtful whether Rimsky-Korsakov was consciously quoting Ex. 60 (a) in Volkhova's lullaby in the last scene. The connection between the song of Soloveï Budmirovich in the fourth tableau and the chorus of sailors in the fifth provides a similar problem. If these similarities were confined to a single work one would naturally accept them as intentional (and rather subtle) devices to give it unity. Recurring in one opera after another, they seem only to betoken poverty of invention, inability to do much more than ring the changes on a few highly original ideas and on others, like Ex. 49 (a), directly borrowed from folk-song.

But the tendency to succumb to the tyranny of an idea, and to repeat it unmercifully with little variation, is perhaps a Russian characteristic allied with that other tendency to think in circles about a point, rather than in a straight line, which we have already noticed. Tolstoy hammers home his theory of history, of the "great men" subordinated to the will of the masses, in much the same way in "War and Peace." It is certainly one of Rimsky-Korsakov's most characteristic mental traits, for he constantly repeats not only themes and characters but even scenes and dramatic situations in later works, with only slight modifications. It is impossible to see and hear the second tableau of "Sadko," for instance—Sadko wandering on the shore of Lake Ilmen in the summer night, singing to his *gusli* accompaniment, and the appearance of Volkhova and her sisters—without thinking of Levko and the russalkas in "May Night." As Van der Pals says, "The second tableau of 'Sadko' appears in both action and music to be a later and riper companion-piece to the russalka scene in 'May Night.'"* But when he goes on to say that all the harmonic, colouristic and romantic elements which only appear in germ form in the earlier work, here come to full flower, it is less easy to agree with him. The

* "N. A. Rimsky-Korssakow: Opernschaffen."

"Sadko" scene is far more elaborate, the handling more skilful, but it is questionable whether the essence of the music shows any greater maturity, any sign that the composer's musical thought, as opposed to his mere technical skill, had advanced at all in the course of seventeen years.

The music of the fantastic scenes, this one by the lakeside and the more elaborate sequence centring about the sixth tableau, the scene in the Sea King's realm, is written in two styles—graceful, lyrical (predominantly vocal) love-music and brilliant highly chromatic, orchestral tone-painting (or, rather, pattern drawing) of the kind Rimsky-Korsakov made peculiarly his own. The artificiality noticeable in "Christmas Eve" reaches a more advanced stage of development in "Sadko." Rimsky-Korsakov was probably right when he said he had never written anything better of its kind; the orchestration is particularly gorgeous. But the actual substance of the music, the framework on which the colour has to be laid, consists of brittle nothings, diatonic commonplaces disguised by the sharpening or flattening of one degree of the scale (usually by sharpening the fifth). It is a curious paradox that this fantastic music of Rimsky-Korsakov's is actually the most coldly calculated. Like his scale of alternate tones and semitones it is, in conception, purely paper music, springing from no natural impulse to create, expressing nothing, communicating no emotion—only tickling the ear with its pungency and unusualness. Nor do these artificial fragments of theme act in the composer's mind like the irritant inserted in the pearl-oyster's shell, serving as the nucleus about which the play of his musical imagination can create genuinely living music. Take this theme, from the procession of the sea monsters in the sixth tableau :—

Ex. 61.

derived from an earlier choral phrase of the sea nymphs and set against the characteristic tone-semitone scale background. It is nothing as it stands, a mere pretext for orchestral colour, but in the minds of some composers it would have generated a natural continuation—and the music would have sprung to life. But Rimsky-Korsakov is content simply to repeat the two bars without alteration and then exactly to repeat all four a fourth higher.

The artificiality of the music can be justified here; its cold sensuousness and glittering emptiness match the world of unreal beings in which Sadko finds himself. Yet the purely intellectual spinning of music in this way, the laying of one little self-contained block of sound against another, the mechanical sense of progress obtained by systematic modulation through cycles of keys, rising or falling regularly in major or minor thirds, the failure of the music to generate a vital impulse from its own nature—all this is frequently characteristic of Rimsky-Korsakov's music even when he is not deliberately aiming at unreality and insubstantiality. (It is very noticeable in the early "Serbian Fantasia.") The non-musician is seduced by the brilliant colours and his ear intrigued by the curious melodic intervals and the pungency of the continual succession of augmented and diminished triads. And the musician, who might be expected to detect the emptiness of all this, is too dazzled by the play of the composer's mind in the manipulation of themes and the contrivance of harmonic subtleties to notice it. It *is* marvellous, this music; no other composer has ever produced anything quite like it. *Mathematical imagination*, if one can speak of such a quality, is the only term which describes the nature of Korsakov's musical thought in these pages of "Sadko" and similar ones in other works. It is a sort of chess in terms of sound, and communicates hardly any more æsthetic emotion. The more genuine physical excitement of the storm must impress every hearer, though it can hardly be compared with that of Borodin's Polovtsian dances, for instance. Yet this storm is merely an amplification of the corresponding section of the early symphonic poem, a fact not without significance (though it would be unwise to attach too much importance to it.)

Against the background of such a pageant of sound, coldly brilliant and racily alive by turns, but painted throughout in the brightest colours, the figures of Volkhova and Sadko himself, to say nothing of the mournful Lyubava and the incidental minor characters, are dwarfed to insignificance. In spite of the beauty of the love-music, some of the best Rimsky-Korsakov ever wrote, and the sensitive charm of such music as that in which Sadko tells the assembled merchants how, if he were rich enough, he would buy one-and-thirty fair ships, freight them with all the wares of Novgorod and sail through all the seas of the world for trade and adventure—in spite of all the delightful music centring about his person, Sadko remains less a character than a symbol. He symbolises, of course, the power of art. Like Levko and Lel he is able, by the magic of his music, to gain admission to the supernatural world (or, rather, to a world in which the powers of nature, taking human form as in the old myths, are accessible to normal intercourse). And not only admission to it, but a certain power over it. This world of illusion, where he mingles with the forces of nature almost like one of themselves, is as real for him and for every artist as the human world of everyday life. He is equally at home in either, and though his immersion in dreams sometimes makes him cold and heartless in his human relationships, he is able to enrich the world of men by the magic gold he wins from the supernatural world. This theme constantly recurs in one form or another in Rimsky-Korsakov's work. Fevronya in "Kitezh" is just such another intermediary between man and nature, except that her power is that of love, not of art. If Sadko seems to be a reincarnation of Lel, Volkhova likewise recalls

Snegurochka, another daughter of a nature-power. She even shares the Snow Maiden's fate—by melting! The composer himself pointed out the similarity of both to the queen of the russalkas in "May Night" and to the shade of the Princess Mlada (who is dead before the opera begins and only appears as a spirit), "visionary female figures who sing and vanish." But Rimsky-Korsakov's symbolism is never very thoroughly worked out, even in "Kitezh' where it is most obvious. In "Sadko" it merely provides a little intellectual ballast to a fairy-tale epic which is perfectly comprehensible without it.

XII.—"THE TSAR'S BRIDE."

"THE first act of 'The Tsar's Bride' contains several unfortunately dry passages perhaps, but after the opening scene of the second act, which is written with a practised hand, the interest of the action increases, and in the fourth act the moving lyrical drama attains a high degree of tension. 'The Tsar's Bride' is exceptionally grateful from the singer's point of view. The scoring and working-out of the accompaniment are effective and not without interest, although the voice parts always predominate and the orchestra employed is only the normal one. . . ." The critic who thus impartially sums up the merits and defects of Rimsky-Korsakov's "Tsarskaya Nevesta," allowing a fairly ample balance in the composer's favour, goes on to reveal his identity and his freedom from false modesty in the following sentences. "The composition of the ensemble pieces, the quartet in the second act and the sextet in the third, particularly interested me as it was a new kind of task. In my opinion operatic ensembles with such polished and independent part-writing have not been composed since Glinka's time." Indeed it was just this desire to try his hand at extended arias and concerted vocal numbers in the old Italian style, "not merely the accidental, more or less fleeting concatenations of voice parts imposed by the modern conception of 'dramatic truth,' according to which two or three characters must never be allowed to sing at the same time," it was this dilettantish spirit of experiment which seems to have finally prompted Rimsky-Korsakov to make an operatic setting of Mey's play. The possibility of turning to account this typically operatic tragedy of passion, jealousy and potions, which Borodin had considered and rejected years before, had occurred to him at least as early as 1891, but it was not until 1898, immediately after the completion of the short "Vera Sheloga" (the reconstructed prologue to "Pskovityanka," also by Mey), that the composition was actually begun. I. F. Tyumenev was entrusted with the task of altering and adding to the original text so as to afford the necessary opportunities for arias and concerted numbers, and the work was composed very rapidly, and partly orchestrated, in the course of the summer.

Rimsky-Korsakov's reversion to a more conventional operatic style than he had as yet written in, after the composition of such a finished masterpiece as "Sadko," can be explained but remains no less difficult to understand. He seems to have been discouraged by his own success, to have felt that in the purely national vein, in epic-fantastic opera, he would never be able to surpass "Sadko." And so in the six or seven years before he returned to it in "Kitezh" we find him experimenting in all directions, though with conspicuous lack of success. In the one act "Mozart and Salieri" (1897) he goes right back to "The Stone Guest" and dramatic truth. "Vera Sheloga" (spring of 1898) is naturally an attempt to recapture the style of "Pskovityanka"—Dargomïzhsky tinctured with lyricism. "The Tsar's Bride" is a hybrid, the old operatic convention of the first half of the nineteenth century decked out with Wagnerian leit-motives and Dargomïzhskian "melodic recitative" and mildly flavoured here and there with the Russian folk-idiom. In 1899 Rimsky-Korsakov returned in "Tsar Saltan" to purely national, fantastic opera, but emphasising the humorous rather than the epic elements and paying more attention to fineness of detail than to breadth. Then came "Servilia" (1900) and "Pan Voevoda" (1903), which may be described as Wagner-and-water, and "Kashcheï the Immortal" (1901), another hybrid in which Wagner is crossed with the "miniature style" of "Tsar Saltan" and the later "Golden Cockerel." Van der Pals, one of Rimsky-Korsakov's apologists, has put forward the specious defence that this wandering in the wilderness was "a necessary intermediate stage in the composer's artistic and spiritual development. To reach his goal, to be able to express the future mission of his people" (in plain English, to write "Kitezh"), "it was necessary for Rimsky-Korsakov to tear his imagination from macrocosmic views and ideas of periods long past and, at any rate for a time, to busy himself with the microcosmic, with the artistic analysis of individual soul-life." There are certainly signs that these experiments in more genuinely dramatic music bore fruit in "Kitezh" but unfortunately the quantity of seed is out of all proportion to the crop. We shall be on safer ground if we assume that Rimsky-Korsakov, with characteristic intellectual restlessness, was amusing himself by trying his strength in new directions, as he actually confesses to doing in "The Tsar's Bride."

The composer tells us in his memoirs that when, after the completion of "Sadko," he composed four songs to poems by Alexey Tolstoy—the first he had written for a long period, he found that the melodies came to him quite otherwise than before. Whereas in his earlier songs the melodies had occurred to him as quasi-instrumental ideas, often conditioned by the harmonic basis which he had conceived first, they now took a purely vocal form. He realised that this was "the only way to write genuine vocal music" and the immediate consequences were a number of settings of A. Tolstoy, Maykov and Pushkin, and "Mozart and Salieri." "The Tsar's Bride" was the first large-scale work in which Rimsky-Korsakov could employ his new vocal style. And at the same time he had in his mind an extraordinary idea, reported by Yastrebtsev, of the possibility of "reconciling Wagner with Glinka, or rather even Wagner with Bellini." It is hardly to be wondered that "The Tsar's Bride," though the best of Rimsky-Korsakov's experimental operas and the only one which ever attained popularity, is something less than a masterpiece.

It is clear that Rimsky-Korsakov, in spite of the candour with which he judged his own music, was often unable to distinguish between intention and achievement. He admitted the "dry passages" in the first act of "The Tsar's Bride," probably because he found the composition of them rather heavy going, but he evidently mistook fluency for inspiration. Usually self-conscious and over-intellectual in the process of composition, he now wrote in a more normal way perhaps for the first time since "Snegurochka." The stream of music flowed so easily that he never noticed how thin it was. "The Tsar's Bride" was at the same time an experiment and a relaxation, some parts of it "written with a practised hand," others by a hand practising new and amusing tricks. Unfortunately, the composer being in a hurry, the practised hand wrote too easily and the practising one avoided difficulties. The subject was there ready-made, a fully developed drama like "Pskovityanka," not a fairy-tale or a village incident waiting for music to cover its bare bones with flesh and blood. On this smooth track Rimsky-Korsakov's mind appears to have moved so easily and rapidly that large stretches of "The Tsar's Bride" are to all intents and purposes *im-*

provised music. "Snegurochka" was also composed very rapidly, it is true, but in that case Korsakov had accumulated a large reservoir of ideas, inspirations of his own and borrowings from the treasury of folk-music, before he began the actual composition.

"The Tsar's Bride" contains only one folk-song, the favourite "Slava" tune which is employed as the motif of Ivan the Terrible, and the former purist in the treatment of folk-melodies so completely forgot his principles that he allowed himself to torture it into duple time in the prelude to Act III :—

Ex. 62.

At the end of Act III, when Malyuta announces the Tsar's intention of marrying Marfa, the "Slava" theme is combined with the "Ivan the Terrible"

motif from "Pskovityanka" (Ex. 35). But this freedom of the score from self-conscious nationalism, in conjunction with the more or less improvised nature of so much of the music, gives the work a peculiar interest from a critical point of view. It affords a unique opportunity of testing the quality of Rimsky-Korsakov's natural musical thought, of watching the stream of his musical consciousness at the average moment. When a composer's writing outpaces the intellectual processes of revision and elaboration we can observe the mysterious spurts and floods, which we call "inspiration," in this stream of thought and the blocks and stoppages when the composer simply carries on with the aid of familiar technical processes, as well as the normal quality of the current, much more clearly than we can see them in work made with an infinity of pains. In this instance, it gives us a chance to discover to what extent the folk-song element had really become absorbed into Rimsky-Korsakov's musical mentality, conscious imitation apart.

The folk-songish passages in "The Tsar's Bride" are for the most part limited to self-contained numbers: the choral "Song of the Hop," Lyubasha's unaccompanied solo, Sobakin's song behind the scenes in the second act, the chorus of Oprichniki at the end of the same act, Domna Saburova's song of the falcon and the swan. And, with the exception of Lyubasha's lovely song in the æolian mode :—

Ex. 63.

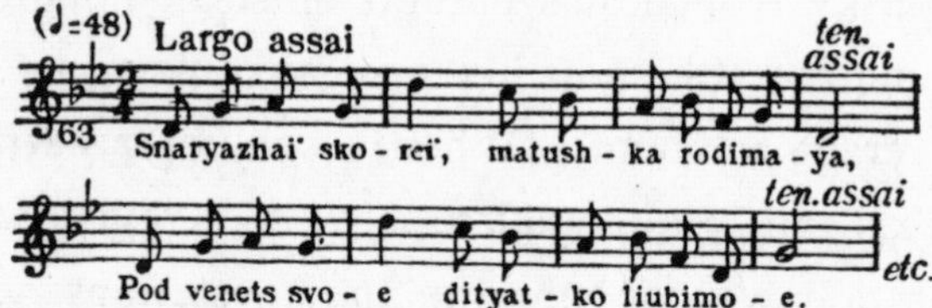

they are all rather flavourless. In one or two other little snatches of tune—the orchestral phrase which heralds the "Hop" chorus, the short *allegro* passage in the middle of Marfa's aria, the orchestral introduction to the sextet—there is more of the genuine tang of folk-music. The characteristics of Rimsky-Korsakov's melodic thought are still present in even the most insipid passages of "The Tsar's Bride," but so mingled with platitudes and emasculated by banal rhythmic transformations that they are hardly recognisable. There is an example of this in the opening of Lïkov's aria, "Storm clouds flying away," inserted in the third act after the first performance at the request of the singer,

Sekar-Rozhansky, because his part was "so poor from the musical point of view":—

Ex. 64.

It begins with the familiar first three notes of Ex. 49 (a), as the first phrase of Ex. 63 ends with them. But how different the effect is here in another rhythm and context. Nothing could be more commonplace. Ex. 64 sounds like a feeble echo of Vakula's insipid love-making in the second scene of "Christmas Eve" (Ex. 44). The original folk-songish pattern has lost every trace of its parentage. On the other hand Lyubasha's lament, unaccompanied throughout, will bear comparison with any of Rimsky-Korsakov's other essays in this genre. It contains no new musical elements, but the old ones are so transmuted that one does not feel the composer is merely serving up a re-hash of familiar ingredients, as he only too often does.

The chief melody of Marfa's big aria in the second act, the finest thing in the opera, also belongs to a familiar type in Rimsky-Korsakov's music and stands out as one of the finest examples of the type :—

Ex. 65.

(She sees "as if it were now, the green garden where with dear friends we used to play.") It is one of Rimsky-Korsakov's most spontaneous inspirations, long-breathed, each curve flowering naturally and inevitably into the next. Ernest Newman was hardly exaggerating when he called it "one of the purest and profoundest expressions of purely melodic ecstasy in the whole of music." There are few more poignant moments in Russian opera than that when in the last act this melody steals back on the clarinet as the background to the unhappy girl's delirium. But the beauty of these one or two outstanding passages only serves to emphasise the insipidity of the music as a whole.

And "The Tsar's Bride" is hardly stronger dramatically than it is lyrically. It is significant that the most gripping effect in the work is produced by

MUSSORGSKY.

means of pure musical beauty. Rimsky-Korsakov can make nothing very remarkable of the dying girl's hallucinations *directly*, as a genuinely dramatic composer would do. He moves us by the contrast between what we see on the stage and the happy past of which the orchestra reminds us—and by the ideal loveliness of the melody itself. The composer opens his first act quite promisingly from a dramatic point of view. Gryaznoy is discovered alone, brooding, and the opening phrase, his leit-motif :—

Ex. 66.

admirably suggests both the man and his mood. (Incidentally, nothing could demonstrate more clearly the way in which Korsakov's mind tended to work in fixed melodic grooves than the almost-identity of the motif (a) with part of Ex. 65, where there can be no question of intentional resemblance.) The musical development of the whole of this first scene from Gryaznoy's motif—both melody and accompaniment of his aria, as well as the orchestral commentary on his recitative monologue—is ingenious, if a little "dry" as the composer confessed. Though the scene is not dramatically gripping, it strikes the right note. One feels that genuine drama may develop at any moment. But it never does. With the entry of Lïkov and the absurd villain Bomelius (whom we have already met in the last scene of "Pskovityanka"), and the fugal chorus of the Oprichniki, the first act lapses into old-fashioned, conventional opera—and not very good conventional opera at that. The aeroplane has taxied very well, but instead of rising it has stopped dead. After that we get nothing more than isolated dramatic moments; and the most striking of these, the scene in the third act where Ivan the Terrible makes his only oppearance on the stage throughout the opera, owes little to the music. The effect of the unseen Tsar overshadowing the visible actors is used to a different end in "The Tsar's Bride" but no less impressively than in "Pskovityanka." His regal motif keeps him musically in one's mind and this single silent appearance gives his shadow a cogency it would lack otherwise.

But there is no blinking the fact that Rimsky-Korsakov, although during the last decade and a half of his life he adopted the career of opera-manufacturer as definitely and exclusively as any Bellini or Rossini or Verdi, was not a true dramatic composer at all. The musical expression of emotion of any kind was not his *forte* and to find music for the crude clash of feeling, the broad sweep of emotion, demanded by the theatre was altogether beyond him, except at a few inspired moments. Nor had he as part of his ordinary equipment anything like Mussorgsky's subtle psychological insight. Here again the few happy exceptions in 'Pskovityanka" and "Kitezh" only emphasise the rule. Given a fairy-tale or village legend, Rimsky-Korsakov could dwell at length on every incident, expanding its essence with lyrical or picturesque music, overlaying it with inessential but wholly delightful detail, and building up a perfectly satisfying, self-contained dream-world of his own. In this half or wholly fantastic type of opera, so peculiarly Russian, he could be himself throughout, or almost throughout. However badly he managed the love-making, it was soon over and the adventures began again. But in "The Tsar's Bride," and other later works, he had hardly any opportunity to be himself. Given a fully developed drama, an infinitely better subject from the point of view of the normal operatic composer, he had neither the ability to identify himself with the different characters nor even the instinct for writing the kind of music which really intensifies a stage situation. Marfa is the only character in the play who is really portrayed in the music associated with her. And she is less a character than a type, one more of Rimsky-Korsakov's naïve, submissive heroines and quite indistinguishable from, say, Olga in "Pskovityanka." It is significant that the parts of "The Tsar's Bride" where Rimsky-Korsakov is most himself are purely lyrical ones where the action is at a standstill, passages like the "Slava" and "Hop" choruses, Lyubasha's song, and the bridal song in the third act, inessential to the action and which naturally hold it up. But the greater part of the play, being true drama—very theatrical drama, neither gave Rimsky-Korsakov opportunities to write the sort of music natural to him nor naturally suggested *any* kind of music to him. And so for long stretches he was, apparently unconsciously, impaled on the horns of the Voltairean dilemma, "the necessity of saying something and the perplexity of having nothing to say."

XIII.—"KITEZH."

STUDY and enjoyment of Rimsky-Korsakov's last opera but one are somewhat hampered by the feeling that too much has been claimed for it. "Kitezh" is one of the composer's most characteristic scores. It contains some of his best music. If he had not written "Snegurochka" and one had forgotten "Sadko," one might more readily agree that "Kitezh" is Korsakov's finest opera. But to speak of it as "the Russian 'Parsifal,'" as some critics have done, is to invite a comparison it will hardly bear—and to draw attention to one or two superficial points of resemblance in some of the musical ideas. The two works really have nothing in common except their general Christian tendency. The relationship of the natural Christian individual (Fevronya and Parsifal) to the orthodox Christian community (the people of Kitezh and the Knights of the Grail) is quite different in the two operas. The sentimental, typically Wagnerian idea of redemption through another has no place in "Kitezh." Grishka Kuterma is not redeemed by or through Fevronya; she can only show him how to save himself.

From a non-musical point of view "Kitezh" is unquestionably the profoundest of Rimsky-Korsakov's operas, a fitting crown to a life-work. In it the composer finds an unexpected, yet apparently from his own point of view satisfying, resolution of his spiritual discord. He shows us a reconciliation of his pantheism, his love of nature and natural forces, his healthy "yea-saying" to life, with something very like orthodox Christianity. The maiden Fevronya evidently embodies the power of universal love. When Prince Vsevolod finds her in the first scene, she is surrounded by birds, with a young bear at her feet, and is examining the wounds of an elk. She loves all living things, fears and hates nothing. Yet this universal love is a sort of innocent paganism, rooted in intense joy of living, in keenest and purest delight of the senses. She rejoices in light and warmth, the colours of the flowers and the thousand mysterious voices of the forest, "not knowing in which the day is brighter or the sun warmer, in dreams or in life." When she speaks of dreams and mysterious voices, Vsevolod, educated in the orthodox faith, is disquieted, and tells her that the wise men of Kitezh teach differently, that dreams are illusions. "One must seek the truth." When he asks her if she goes to pray in the churches, she answers simply, "No. Is not God everywhere?" and in a mystical ecstasy goes on to sing—significantly to a melody of the Russian church—her confession of faith: the forest itself is a church, and day and night there goes up from it a hymn of praise, all the voices of the beasts and birds continually glorifying their Maker. And finally she seems to place beside God, *zemlya matushka*, the Earth Mother. Vsevolod again thoughtfully contrasts her belief with the teaching he has been accustomed to hear, that one can only gain Heaven by turning one's back on earthly joys, and he feels that she is right. In a third song Fevronya, after reaffirming her faith in universal love and forgiveness, goes on to prophesy the coming of a millennium which shall be simply an endless spring idyll, a naïve and delightful conception of an earthly paradise full of flowers and birds.

So far everything is quite comprehensible, but at this point the young Prince dispels the transcendental atmosphere by ecstatically proposing marriage in the conventional operatic way. The motivation of the rest of the opera is never quite clear. Perhaps we may put it that the artistic vitality of the work was too much for its ethical content. Fevronya goes out into the world, showing the same patience, love and forgiveness in the face of every trial. It is apparently through her prayers that the city of Kitezh is made invisible and saved from the Tartars. Yet when at the end of her ordeal her prophecy comes true (the poetic symbol of her death) and an unnatural spring returns to the earth, lighted candles appear on the trees and the forest birds find words, it is her dead lover, the son of orthodoxy, who appears, giving her bread and telling her that whosoever eats it shall have everlasting joy (not "everlasting life"), and who leads her to the Invisible City. The dialogue in the last scene between the Maiden and the old Prince Yury suggests that Rimsky-Korsakov was thinking not so much of an orthodox heaven beyond the clouds as of the earth in some future age, transfigured by human love and compassion, a world peopled with Dostoevskian Myshkins. "Dreams have become realities. What before was only thought is here alive," says the old Prince, and Fevronya is told that she is worthy to live in the transfigured Kitezh because of three gifts she has brought to God : her dove-like gentleness, her loving kindness and her compassionate tears.

Fevronya is clearly Rimsky-Korsakov's ideal Christian, who understands the truths hidden from the wisest of the orthodox teachers. The orthodox community is saved through her prayers. But the composer can hardly have meant by his conclusion that, in turn, the intervention of the orthodox was necessary for *her* salvation. Perhaps he was merely stating his belief that orthodox and unorthodox alike are travelling to the same goal. Fevronya seems to embody the fusion of everything good in the old nature-worship with the purest essence of Christianity, but Rimsky-Korsakov has merely shown her as reconciled with orthodoxy—without showing *how*. He could claim that he was under no obligation to do so, being an artist, not a religious teacher. But "Kitezh," though it may be "first and foremost a *musical* work," as the composer says in his preface to the score, is obviously intended to have a significance other than a purely artistic one. And the very fact that this inner significance is unclear, mystical and illogical, points to a radical change in Rimsky-Korsakov's thought at this period of his life.

It is unfortunate, though perhaps not without significance, that the composer's memoirs, so full of details concerning the planning and composition of the earlier operas, give only the barest records of the writing of "Kitezh" and not a word concerning the ideas at the back of it. Apparently Rimsky-Korsakov first thought of combining the two legends of "The Invisible City of Kitezh" and of "St. Fevronya of Murom" in a single opera soon after the finishing touches had been put to "The Tsar's Bride."* He notes that in the winter of 1898-9, while he and Belsky were preparing the scenario of "The Legend of Tsar Saltan," they discussed this as well as other possible operatic subjects: Byron's "Heaven and Earth," which he kept in mind till the end of his life, and the "Nausicaa" episode from the "Odyssey," to which in 1901 he wrote a choral prologue, published separately as "A Page of Homer," Op. 60. "Tsar Saltan" was followed by two of Rimsky-Korsakov's

---

* Yastrebtsev says he had discussed the suitability of the Kitezh legend as the subject of a symphonic poem as early as 1892.

weakest operas, "Servilia" and "Pan Voevoda," and the short "Kashcheï the Immortal," interesting for its advanced harmony and as the high-water mark of Wagner's influence on Rimsky-Korsakov, but of no great musical value. But all this time the idea of "Kitezh" was maturing in the composer's mind. In the spring of 1903, before "Pan Voevoda" was finished, he began to make sketches for the first act of the "Legend." Belsky prepared the libretto in the summer of that year, discussing even the most insignificant details with the composer. By the end of the summer Korsakov had composed the first act and both tableaux of the fourth; on his return to Petersburg for the winter, he sketched out the second act and the first tableau of the third. The score of "Kitezh" was finished during the summer of 1904 at Vechasha. That is all the composer is disposed to tell us about a work which appears to be the result of some spiritual crisis and which, if the claims of its admirers are not greatly exaggerated, must have been written in a white-heat of inspiration. Rimsky-Korsakov has told us about the almost clairvoyant condition in which he composed "Snegurochka" and, in considerable detail, of his rather less intense excitement during the writing of "Sadko," but he dismisses "Kitezh" as if it were of no more importance than "Servilia" or "Pan Voevoda." It is true the whole of the latter part of the memoirs is somewhat scant of detail, as if the writer were weary of his self-imposed task and could bring no interest to the retailing of the events of only a year or two before. Yet none of the other operas is passed over as curtly as "Kitezh."

From a purely musical point of view "Kitezh" is at the same time a step backward and a summing-up. After "Sadko" Rimsky-Korsakov, as we have seen, had for a time abandoned the folkish-fantastic style of which he was a complete master for a more conventionally dramatic type in which he was reduced to the level of an unversed apprentice. Undecided in musical method, wavering between predominantly *sung* opera, as in "The Tsar's Bride," and almost pure Wagnerian declamation, as in "Kashcheï," he had also been trying to cure his music of its Russian accent, its principal charm, for the sake of "freedom of style." Neither "Servilia" nor "Pan Voevoda" has anything like the dramatic power of the last scene of "The Tsar's Bride," and the stream of lyrical inspiration runs through them even thinner. Of the seven operas written between "Sadko" and "Kitezh" only "Tsar Saltan" is written consistently in the national idiom. In "Saltan" the striving for drama and psychological subtlety is temporarily relaxed; the composer is content once more merely to tell a Russian fairy-tale; and in consequence "Saltan" is musically a sheer delight. But it was not till he wrote "Kitezh" that Rimsky-Korsakov regained the level of "Sadko."

"Kitezh" is composed in the contrasted styles of which Rimsky-Korsakov was so fond, the harmonically piquant but essentially artificial music usually associated with the fantastic and supernatural elements being replaced by barbaric pseudo-Tartar music of a very similar nature. The folk-songish music of the "Russian" scenes differs in no respect from that in the earlier operas. Indeed the score contains hardly any fresh elements. Even the melodies borrowed or imitated from the music of the Russian church have precursors in "Sadko" (the appearance of St. Nicholas), "Tsar Saltan" (chorus at the end of Act II), and "Christmas Eve." Nor can it be said that the experiments of the dramatic operas bore much fruit in "Kitezh." There is a certain advance in the expressive power of the vocal music, it is true; and the treatment of Grishka Kuterma, his impudence, the torment of his spirit and his growing madness, makes this drunken vagabond one of the most striking and psychologically convincing characters in the whole range of Rimsky-Korsakov's operas. Yet Grishka cuts a more ordinary figure when compared with the characters of Mussorgsky's world. After all, his portrait (though more elaborate) is no more cleverly drawn than that of the terrible Tsar in Korsakov's own "Pskovityanka." The mere fact that he is alive at all, a human being with a battered human soul, not a mere type or character in a fairy-tale, throws him into relief against the background of unreal and half-real creatures who people so much of Korsakov's dramatic work. He is a symbol, but something more substantial as well. And the same may be said of Fevronya herself. Though she conforms superficially to Rimsky-Korsakov's favourite type of passive heroine, whose only characteristics are patience and forgiveness, she is far more positive and definite than any of the Olgas and Marfas and Militrissas of the earlier operas. One little trait after another gives her sharper definition and deeper individuality, till near the end when, having taken the bread of everlasting joy, she throws the crumbs to the birds and she and her lover set out hand in hand on their journey to the Invisible City to the sound of twitterings and cuckoo-calls, she stands out as one of the most memorable figures in the whole of operatic literature. Vsevolod is a poor thing to mate with her. He is the conventional tenor hero to the life—or, rather, in the lack of it. When Fedor Poyarok brings to Great Kitezh the false report that it is Fevronya who has betrayed the city, her lover, though he seems to believe the story without question, only remarks *poco agitato*, "What? What, *she?* O God, be merciful!"—and leaves it at that! His father, the old Prince Yury, is the personification of priesthood, and the simple music associated with him is deeply impressive. But the other characters are of little account. Bedyay and Bouroundy, the Tartar chiefs, belong to the slightly comic world of Fafner and Fasolt; it is impossible to believe that they are the terrible figures they are intended to be. They will not bear comparison in any respect with Borodin's Konchak.

But "Kitezh" is, even more than most operas, "first and foremost a musical work." Its characters live and its religious message has meaning only in so far as they are enveloped and expressed in living music. Fevronya, in particular, is a purely musical character. That is to say, she is not a woman completely drawn and then set to music as Isolde or Brünnhilde is. She is like Mozart's heroines in that all, or at any rate the most important part, of what we know of her, is told us only by her music. Her music develops from a few simple germs and the rest of the work is formed about it as about a nucleus.

Like "Sadko," "Kitezh" opens with a piece of nature-painting, a vague murmur centring for the most part about a single chord :—

Ex. 67

In "Sadko" it is the confused murmur of the sea, here that of the forest, which sets the pervading mood of the greater part of the work and recurs from time to time throughout it. But instead of breaking off, like the prelude to "Sadko," these *Waldweben*, so like Wagner's as regards the means employed and so unlike in the end attained, lead directly into the first scene and are heard as a background throughout the greater part of Act I. More definite themes are evolved from the vague rustle of the violins, like chaos itself taking shape. Above the divided string tremolo the oboe begins to sing a long-drawn melody expanded from Ex. 67 (a):—

Ex. 68

of which the last two bars are the chief motif of Fevronya herself, so that she is, so to speak, musically identified with the voice of Nature. The essential similarity of this motif to Ex. 48 in "Snegurochka" has already been pointed out. Bird-calls are heard, also recalling "Snegurochka"; more naturalistic, less idealised than the voice of Wagner's "forest bird." And then comes a warm, broad melody in D flat, a "glorification of solitude," as Korsakov called his prelude:—

Ex. 69

When the curtain goes up Fevronya sings Ex. 68, oboe and flute echoing her. Already her musical portrait is beginning to take shape. There is something indescribably moving about the simplicity of Ex. 68. And just as this theme, a variation of the ever-recurring Rimsky-Korsakovian idea, Ex. 49 (b), suggests the passive side of Fevronya's nature, her humility and gentleness and naïveté, the melody of "glorification," Ex. 69, which she now sings in C major, expresses the active side, her warm love for all living things and her dreamy exaltation. Musically it is a not unworthy counterpart to Marfa's great aria in "The Tsar's Bride," though it has not the same sweep and finality. The scene with the birds and animals is developed almost entirely from the separate motives of Ex. 68, interwoven with naïve bird-calls and rhythmic figures associated with the bear and elk. When Fevronya tells the bear that when he is older he will be tamed and taught to dance, the clarinet plays a snatch of melody almost note for note the same as the chief theme of the well-known "Tumblers' Dance" in "Snegurochka."

On the appearance of Vsevolod the texture of the music weakens. The love-music, almost passionless—as ever with Rimsky-Korsakov, is less banal than that which he usually wrote for situations of this kind. Its idyllic purity strikes no note false to the general feeling of the scene. Yet the temperature of the musical inspiration has dropped perceptibly. The music is still derived from Ex. 68, but in its new 6/8 guise it has lost its virtue and drifted dangerously near the commonplace. Only the recurrence of the earlier music leads us back from the world of opera to the world of legend. Gradually fresh themes begin to be associated with the original ones. When Fevronya sings to the Prince of the wonder of the flowers and the mysterious voices of the forest, a new melody delicately outlined by flute and harp is heard over the murmuring semiquavers. And when she tells him that the forest is the vast temple of a divine mystery, a hymn-like melody emerges from Ex. 68 in imitation :—

Ex. 70

and is taken up by Fevronya in a broad, tranquil

alla breve. As she sings with ever-increasing ecstasy of the future world transfigured by universal love, other themes later associated with the Paradise Birds, Sirin and Alkonost, are heard above the rustle of the forest till at the end this vague, continuous undertone takes definite shape (as if a long-held discord had been resolved at last) in a passage which suggests the ringing of innumerable little bells :—

Ex. 71 (a) and (b)

This "carillon of eternal bliss" takes several shapes besides the two quoted here, but its last four notes always remind the hearer of its connection with Fevronya and the murmuring forest.

Later, after Vsevolod's disappearance, the arrival of Poyarok and his men with their lusty folk-song takes one back to Rimsky-Korsakov's earlier operas. At the very end of the act, when they reply to Fevronya's enquiry as to the Prince's identity, a new theme flames out on the trumpets at the word "Kitezh," reminding one of the fanfare-theme associated with the city of Ledenets in "Tsar Saltan."

The second act of "Kitezh" opens with a crowd-scene, a feature of Rimsky-Korsakov's operas almost as inevitable and conventional as the ballet in the operas of pre-Wagnerian days. The scene in Little Kitezh is constructed in the usual way from material of familiar types. The bear-leader's repeated cry to his "Mikhaylushka" and the old *gusli*-player's song are both of the *bïlina*-melody class and the various dance-themes are distractingly like dozens of similar tunes in Rimsky-Korsakov's earlier works. The only fresh feature is the baiting of Grishka Kuterma, who thus makes his first appearance on the scene; his theme, alone of those from which this self-contained interlude is built up, is of importance in the musical architecture of the opera as a whole. It is not till Fevronya appears that the symphonic web begins to develop afresh, first with a motif in 5/8 time to which in the first act

Fevronya has greeted Vsevolod, now in the orchestra and quickly used in counterpoint with Ex. 69. Then in the scene between Grishka and Fevronya we hear still further metamorphoses of Ex. 68 :—

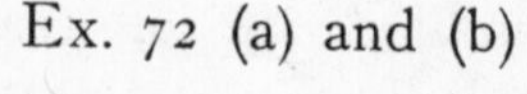

the first when she tells him not to sin, the other when she speaks of the humility proper to a maiden.

The irruption of the Tartars introduces a fresh group of themes : first, a motif of the conventional "barbaric and threatening" type which, having no

Ex. 73

real musical vitality of its own, is easily twisted into any number of shapes, equally meaningless, without violence to its nature. Then, more directly associated with the two chiefs, the old Tartar song, "On the river Darya" (Ex. 73), links this last but one of Rimsky-Korsakov's great works with his first, for the *andante* of his First Symphony is based on this very tune.* A third Tartar theme, sung by the two chiefs in thirds :—

Ex. 74

is actually another version of the same song,† though

* This was the "Russian theme" which he tells us was sent him by Balakirev and on which he wrote the *andante* while his ship, the "Almaz," was lying in the Thames during the winter of 1861-2. "I composed it without a piano," he says. "We hadn't one on the vessel; perhaps once or twice I played through what I had written in some river-side beer-shop." The history of music records few incongruities more pleasant than this—the first performance of parts of the first Russian symphony on the piano of a Thames-side public house. The melody was evidently a favourite of Rimsky-Korsakov's, for he made a choral setting of it in 1876.

† Both songs, with yet a third melody to the same words, are given in Rimsky-Korsakov's "Hundred Russian Folk-Songs." All three were taken down by Balakirev from the singing of P. Yakushkin.

Van der Pals* curiously enough takes it for "a variation or, more correctly, a distortion of the carillon theme" (that is, of Ex. 71b), an example of the pitfalls which beset the path of the too ingenious analyst.

The phrase to which Fevronya sings her prayer, "Lord, make invisible the town of Kitezh," which plays such an important part in the next act, might also be considered a variation of the carillon motif, though they really have nothing more in common than the fact that both are based on the same formula as the bell-theme in "Parsifal." The whole of the first tableau of the third act, the midnight scene in Great Kitezh itself, belongs to the same mental world. Here Rimsky-Korsakov does really seem to be breaking fresh ground. The music, above all in the long monologue of the old Prince Yury, has a mystic depth—attained by the simplest means—quite without parallel in any of his other works. Only in the continually recurring "Kitezh" fanfare, the folk-songish flavour of the choral greeting to Poyarok and the vivid tone-painting which accompanies the youth's first narration can we recognise the characteristic Rimsky-Korsakov.

* "N. A. Rimsky-Korssakow; Opernschaffen."

The beautiful long-drawn melody of the youth's second narration ("Woe, woe to the city of Kitezh! The crosses are gone from the domes of the churches"):—

Ex. 75

reminds one (in feeling, not melodically) of the unaccompanied chorus of peasants in "Prince Igor." The cadential pattern (a) is noticeable in several themes in "Kitezh"—the men's chorus at the end of Act I, the leit-motif of Poyarok, and others; it may have been unconsciously derived from the end of Ex. 68. Here in Act III it recurs in the finely conceived chorus of Vsevolod and the Kitezh warriors as they go out to battle, irresistibly reminding one of the similar scene of Tucha and his followers in "Pskovityanka." Their song fades away into the music of the transformation scene, a wonderful piece of sensuous sound dominated by the theme of Fevronya's prayer and (as the bells begin to ring of their own accord) the carillon of endless bliss.

The interlude leading to the second tableau of this act, "The Battle of Kerzhenets," is sometimes performed as a separate concert-piece, though the playing off of the chorus of the Kitezh warriors against the various Tartar themes and Korsakov's stereotyped "ride" figure (as used in "Christmas Eve," for instance) is not very interesting. Like the other big orchestral interlude in "Kitezh," the "Journey to the Invisible City" in the last act, it reveals all Korsakov's typical weaknesses as a symphonic writer, in particular his inability to build except by the primitive method of laying blocks of sound end to end.

The second tableau takes us back to Fevronya and Grishka, from the epic to the psychological. These two have already confronted each other, but now for the first time they are alone together. The juxtaposition throws an ever more and more piercing light on the character of each. Grishka's mind is already beginning to give way. The sound of the bells of the city he has betrayed rings ceaselessly in his ears. (And now we do really hear a "distortion" of the carillon theme.) Gradually his poor, tormented soul is stripped naked before Fevronya, as he cries out in terror and begs her to free him, now wheedling and cringing, now telling her defiantly that life has nothing more to offer her, since he has spread the report that it is she who is the traitor. Then softening before her infinite compassion he pours out the whole of his misery, his grievance against fate and society and himself, half in truth, half in the endeavour to move her to release him through pity, while Fevronya with each reply seems to grow in spiritual stature. The end of the scene, as the first rays of dawn show the reflection of the Invisible City in the waters of the lake, brings the emotional tension to a climax. The real bell-sounds, with the fanfare-motif, alternate with their distortion in Grishka's maddened mind; and his wild laughter as he rushes off, dragging Fevronya with him, is not easily forgotten. Yet even this terrible piece of soul-painting is surpassed in the forest scene of the last act. Up till now we have been witnessing a tragedy, very horrible but of a kind which music can hardly intensify. Unlike Fevronya, Grishka is altogether complete without music. The music adds nothing to his portrait. It matches it but, if the truth must be told, only intermittently helps to deepen its effect. But now Grishka tells Fevronya to pray if she wants to—only "not to *Him*, but to the Earth"—and there is a curiously moving quality in the music of the prayer which this crazed wreck of humanity mutters after her, his mind gradually wandering, till he breaks off and cries out in terror, thinking he sees the Devil himself. The wild music of his dance, as he sings and whistles to appease his tormentor, will bear comparison with Mussorgsky's essays in the macabre—even with Boris's hallucination. Rimsky-Korsakov himself wrote nothing else quite like it, for it is no mere grotesque pattern of sounds. It communicates an authentic shudder of horror. From this point till the end of the tableau Rimsky-Korsakov's musical imagination continued working at full pressure. The hysterical flood of sound as Grishka rushes off, leaving Fevronya to her fate, dies down to the quiet murmur of the forest. And then Fevronya sings a gravely beautiful little lullaby to her tired heart, while harp, glockenspiel and celesta decorate the strangely, disturbingly sweet music of the miraculous transformation with twinkling little points of sound-light. The last motif of Ex. 68 undergoes one final transformation growing out into a magnificent, long-breathed phrase, over mounting violin figures :—

Ex. 76

expressing the exaltation of the girl's soul as it gradually frees itself from the limitations of mortality. The voice of Alkonost tells her of the approach of death, no longer fearful, and just before the appearance of Vsevolod comes a deeply moving passage where the motif to which in the first act she has sung the praise of Mother Earth grows into that of the "glorification of solitude." Now she sings them to welcome "sweet Death, dear guest, my long desired one":—

Ex. 77

As in Act I, the coming of the Prince perceptibly lowers the imaginative temperature of the music until the scene of the mystic giving of bread. Vsevolod's phrase, "Whoso eats of our bread":—

Ex. 78.

(heard already in the third act when Fevronya tells Grishka of the great mystery of God) assumes great importance in the last scene, though it is less impressive in the grandiose form in which it appears there than in this simple one which so perfectly expresses the nature of the most solemn of Christian rites. The final scene in the Invisible City is a marvellous piece of musical fresco painting; not flawless, for not all the material is of equal value and there is a great deal of the usual symmetrical repetition, though the formal, highly stylised character of the whole scene supplies a motive for this other than the customary "purely musical" one. Yet, even in these, perhaps the loftiest pages he ever wrote, Rimsky-Korsakov's creative fire failed to generate enough heat to fuse mere structure into living organism, or rather to fuse all the little separate eight-bar or sixteen-bar organisms into one big one. To say that is not to deny the sustained imagination and all-through impulse which alone could have made such a satisfying synthesis of so many thematic elements: the bells, the fanfare, folk-song and church-melody, the motives of Fevronya and the murmuring forest, and the voices of the mysterious Paradise birds. But music of the level of "Kitezh" can be judged only by the highest standards, and, applying these, it is easy to see that it lacks that spontaneity as a whole of which there is plenty of evidence in the parts, above all in Fevronya's questions and the replies of the other soloists.

We know that Rimsky-Korsakov was a religious sceptic, though as he confessed he had, as an artist, an extraordinary predilection for depicting religious ceremonies. He said of his "Easter Overture" that to understand it "one must have attended a Russian Easter mass in a cathedral, among the closely packed masses of people, during the simultaneous celebration of the mass by numerous priests and deacons." But there was something of the priest about Rimsky-Korsakov himself. One has only to look at his photograph to see that he needed nothing but the dress to turn him in appearance into a typical Orthodox *mitropolit*. It is obvious that "Kitezh" was not conceived objectively as a mere external representation of a belief to which the composer was indifferent or in which he was interested only as an artistic subject. The "Easter Overture" may be such, a purely artistic recollection of mass-excitement and the physical joy of sharing it. But "Kitezh" is so clearly something more than that, that it is impossible not to speculate as to its significance in connection with the composer's own spiritual development. Was the idea of "Kitezh" simply a triumph of instinct over reason? Was Rimsky-Korsakov actually becoming reconciled with orthodox beliefs as he grew older? Or did he and Belsky really think, as it appears, that they had found the essence of Christianity in nature itself? No one can say. The "Legend" is too unclear in thought. But, after all, art is more important than the artist. His personal problems, fascinating as they may be, are of only incidental importance.

XIV.—"THE GOLDEN COCKEREL."

RIMSKY-KORSAKOV'S perverse refusal to round off his career by dying after the composition of "Kitezh" appears to have aroused a slight sense of grievance in more than one critic. "Kitezh" would have been such an appropriate final message to the world that the humour and irony of "The Golden Cockerel" seem to have struck critics as an unpleasant discord sounded after a perfect cadence, almost as a sort of death-bed joke. Yet the "Cockerel" was in no wise the work of a dying man, or even of a very old one; the composer was only sixty-three. It is true the attacks of *angina pectoris* compelled Korsakov to take life easily, but his health became really serious only in December, 1907, after the completion of the "Cockerel" and just six months before his death. The curious point is that after "Kitezh" Rimsky-Korsakov did actually wonder whether the time had not come for him to give up composing. The last page of his autobiography, finished in 1906, is overshadowed by the old fear of becoming a "singer who has lost his voice." And although he was still thinking of further operas and he and Belsky went on discussing plans, Pushkin's "Golden Cockerel" was not one of them. He still kept harking back to the subject of Byron's "Heaven and Earth" (a fact which suggests that the religious trend of his thought in "Kitezh" was no mere episode) and toying with that of the Volga pirate, Stenka Razin, the hero of a symphonic poem by Glazunov. But ideas would not come and, very much as Tchaïkovsky decided that he was played out just before writing "Casse-Noisette," Rimsky-Korsakov seems for a time to have made up his mind that there was nothing left for him but to close his account with the past by restoring some of the cuts in his edition of "Boris," orchestrating a few songs—his own and Mussorgsky's, touching up "Kashcheï" and the short orchestral "Dubinushka," and working at his great book on orchestration. The decision to compose "The Golden Cockerel" was made quite suddenly in September or October, 1906, but when it was taken Korsakov threw himself whole-heartedly into the task and worked at full pressure until it was finished.

It is only natural to compare "The Golden Cockerel" with the "Tsar Saltan" of eight years before. Both are based by Belsky on tales by Pushkin. In each the central figure is a naïve, absurd tsar. Both are composed in Rimsky-Korsakov's so-called "miniature style." But there the parallel ends. Not only is the musical texture of the two operas different, mainly diatonic in "Saltan," predominantly chromatic in the "Cockerel," but the whole point of view is different. In "Saltan" one feels that the composer has identified himself with the childish, dream-like world of the fairy-tale. In none of his fantastic operas does he accept the ridiculous and extraordinary more gravely and matter-of-factly. Much of the charm of the thing is due to this apparent ingenuousness of a narrator who seems to believe every word of the extravagancies he is reciting. But in "The Golden Cockerel" the composer often appears to be standing outside the ridiculous drama and on a more sophisticated plane of thought from which he *sees* that it is ridiculous. In "Saltan" the music is one with the story throughout; in the "Cockerel" it frequently comments on it. The naïve humour of "Saltan" is still present in "The Golden Cockerel" but mingled with it is a strong flavouring of biting, and slightly bitter, wit. When Rimsky-Korsakov wrote music for Saltan he had had one or two brushes with a paternal autocracy, it is true, but they had not been serious. He had suffered nothing worse than the compulsory substitution, on the demand of the censor, of a vague male "highness" for the Empress in "Christmas Eve." But in the interval before he wrote music for Dodon (in 1905, to be exact), there had been an almost-revolution in which the composer had openly sympathised with the wrong side. He had been involved in a warfare of manifestoes and student-demonstrations and had been dismissed from his professorship at the Conservatoire. So when he came to draw Dodon he did so in a less kindly spirit. Autocracy, recognising the caricature, took its revenge by preventing the performance of "The Golden Cockerel" during the composer's lifetime and so hastening his death, it is said, by the annoyance.

Different as "The Golden Cockerel" is from "Kitezh," the two works have this in common—that both hint at some mysterious, hidden meaning which no one has yet managed to elucidate quite satisfactorily. Delightful as "The Golden Cockerel" is as pure nonsense, the prologue with the Astrologer's hint at a moral (together with Rimsky-Korsakov's predilection for symbolism) sets one hunting for a deeper significance in the story. But it is evident from Belsky's preface to the libretto that even he, and presumably Rimsky-Korsakov himself, had failed to see what Pushkin really meant by it. He invents a mythical origin for the story,* which explains nothing, and says that it "draws a lesson from the unhappy consequences of human passions and weaknesses." But beyond the rather obvious lesson that old men are likely to get into trouble if they run after young women, there is not very much to be learned from the opera. In Dodon Pushkin may have been satirising not only autocracy but that typically Russian variety of laziness which, from the hero of Goncharov's famous novel, has become known as "Oblomovism." But the Cockerel itself, which at first seems so obviously the symbol of *something*, cannot be made, except by the most tortuous ingenuity, to symbolise *anything*. When the Astrologer comes forward at the end and tells the

* It seems to be based, he says, on some fabulous attempt of a powerful magician (the Astrologer) to carry off the Queen of the Air (the Queen of Shemakhan) by the aid of a mortal king (Dodon). The attempt failed and the magician consoled himself by inventing the story of the king's ingratitude.

audience that he and the Tsaritsa, who have appeared to be fantastic beings creating confusion in a more or less real world, are actually the only realities and that all the rest is illusion, he only makes the puzzle more bewildering than ever. So one is obliged to conclude, not very satisfactorily, that after all, Queen, Cockerel and Astrologer are simply an elaborate mystification, that there is no moral deeper than the obvious ones, and that the satire is equally superficial, merely adding spice to an ordinary fairy-tale. But it is not unlikely that Rimsky-Korsakov was attracted to the subject in the first place by this suggestion of a deeper meaning, and it is certainly true that he and Belsky (who, as usual, consulted him with regard to every detail) underlined the satirical element and added a touch of malice not in the original.

Musically "The Golden Cockerel" cannot be compared with "Sadko" or "Kitezh" on the one hand, and it owes nothing to "The Tsar's Bride" and the other "vocal" and "dramatic" operas on the other. In the highly chromatic harmonic texture of so many of its pages, its predominantly orchestral nature and the almost unbroken continuity of the music, it resembles "Kashcheï the Immortal,"

Rimsky-Korsakov's nearest approach to pure Wagnerian music-drama, while in other respects, in the style of the recitatives and the dry, humorous characterisation by short-winded folk-songish leitmotives, it is closer to "Tsar Saltan." Stylistically, then, "The Golden Cockerel" lies midway between the two earlier "miniature" operas, both of which it surpasses in achievement. As in the big fantastic operas, a simple, diatonic idiom is contrasted with a more complicated, chromatic one. But whereas in "Sadko," for instance, the two styles are kept more or less separate, one or the other definitely predominating in any scene, in the "Cockerel" they are closely interwoven and the chromatic idiom instead of being the secondary, contrasting element in the music is now the chief one. Though much of the melodic material is diatonic it is enveloped in a web of highly spiced harmony. The purely diatonic style is reserved for one or two unimportant characters, the Tsar's sons and his housekeeper, Amelfa, and for brief episodes like the delightful music which lulls the Tsar to sleep in the first act. The Tsar's own themes, like the foolish old man himself, are continually entangled in the magic chromatic net of the Queen of Shemakhan. The Astrologer's music, continually see-sawing between distant keys (see Ex. 43), is as insubstantial as the sinister figure himself.

In this sort of musical characterisation, Rimsky-Korsakov was a master. Almost incapable of painting a full-length musical portrait, he was peculiarly adept in the musical labelling of characters. Even in his earliest operas we find him striving by no means unsuccessfully to give each character a distinct musical speech. In "Sadko" the hero, who hardly exists at all as a human being seen in the round, is to a certain extent characterised by his distinctive type of recitative. His music tells us nothing about him. It is far from being musical portraiture, as Ivan's music is in "Pskovityanka." Yet it distinguishes him far more satisfactorily than the mere *etiquette* of a leit-motif would do. As a matter of fact, Rimsky-Korsakov's personal leit-motives in most of his operas are not conspicuously successful. Themes as expressive as Fevronya's are exceptional with him; they are usually only more or less striking tags. But the musical characterisation in "The Golden Cockerel" is brilliantly successful. Again there is no question of genuine portraiture, though the fact that the music is associated with persons with sharply defined characteristics instead of with negative, shadowy beings like Snegurochka and Sadko gives it substance and validity. But the leit-motives are extraordinarily apt. Consider these themes associated with the foolish, pompous old Tsar :—

Ex. 79

with the perpetually bad-tempered *voevoda* Polkan :—

Ex. 80

and with the fussy old housekeeper, Amelfa :—

Ex. 81

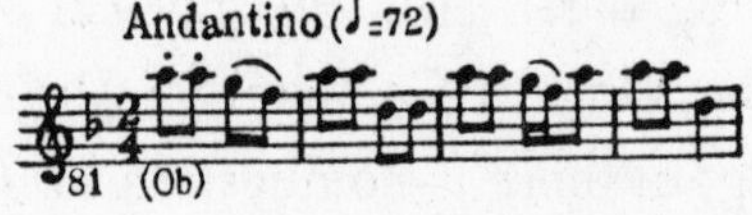

(this last one practically identical with that of the

Novgorod merchants in "Mlada"). Not only are they effective as mere labels but their development is so consistent and so complete, very little of the score being independent of leit-motives, that from beginning to end every character is sharply defined in the music. Again, take the arabesque pattern, perhaps the most important theme in the whole score, associated with the seductive Tsaritsa :—

Ex. 82

Could the coldly sensual, demoniac nature of the woman, her mystery and her insubstantiality, be more strikingly suggested musically? And unlike so many of Korsakov's fantastic themes, it sounds spontaneously created, not consciously invented, in spite of the ease with which it can be made to progress infinitely by minor thirds (a circumstance exploited to the full in the long clarinet cadenza in the prologue) and of the fact that it sounds equally well upside down, as the composer obligingly demonstrates immediately after this cadenza :—

Ex. 83

The almost-identity of the first four notes of Ex. 82 with an important motif in the Astrologer's greeting to the Tsar, and to which he first sings of "my Golden Cockerel," may be intended to hint at the mysterious connection between him, the bird and the Tsaritsa. (Though the song about the Cockerel can hardly have been meant to recall the Hindu merchant in "Sadko"!)

It is easy to see how the extraordinary flexibility of Ex. 82 made it perfect material for Rimsky-Korsakov's peculiarly constituted mind to work on. It can be subjected to almost innumerable metamorphoses without losing its identity or its expressive power, and it lends itself to an infinite play of harmonic and contrapuntal ingenuity—as in this delightful passage at the end of the Tsaritsa's tale of her magic island:—

Ex. 84

And the same is almost equally true of the themes of the Tsar and the Cockerel. Nothing could be more characteristic of Rimsky-Korsakov than the trumpet-fanfares behind the scenes, which follow the Cockerel's alarms in Act I :—

Ex. 85

where the composer's thought-process is the precise equivalent of the substitution of $(x + y)^2$ for $x^2 + 2xy + y^2$ in an equation.

Indeed, "The Golden Cockerel" is perhaps the most elaborately fabricated of all Rimsky-Korsakov's scores. Whatever doubts one feels as to the spontaneity of his inspiration (and as usual the ideas that appear most spontaneous are also the weakest) and the natural vitality of a great deal of the music, there can be no denying the composer's unsurpassed intellectual brilliance in his last composition. Rimsky-Korsakov was always essentially a miniaturist, perhaps—partly by instinct, partly owing to his limitations. Freed from the necessity of filling a huge canvas like the submarine scene of "Sadko," writing for a quickly moving comedy of individuals instead of a static, impersonal epic, the composer could here file away to his heart's content. He does not entirely neglect purely musical symmetry of architecture—in the council of war in the first act, in the sleep episode with the Cockerel's two alarms, in the opening of Act II, and other places, where he takes advantage of the formalised nature of the fairy-tale. But he abandons the attempt to write symphonically—there being no inducement—with happy results. He can lay his finely wrought musical filigree carefully on the incidents of the story, knowing that the story alone will be sufficient to bind it together and give it shape. In some respects he almost seems to have returned to Dargomïzhsky, with his detailed underlining of the action and sharp characterisation of each actor. Indeed, but for the nature of the recitative, slightly stylised to suggest the grotesque nature of the characters, and the predominance of the orchestra (two very important "buts," of course), "The Golden Cockerel" is written more or less according to Dargomïzhskian principles. The "vocal" style is abandoned as completely as the pseudo-symphonic, for even the melodies of the Tsaritsa's songs—her "Hymn to the Sun," for instance—are really instrumental in nature. Actually, of course, Rimsky-Korsakov had not returned to Dargomïzhsky at all. He arrived at the style of "The Golden Cockerel" by way of Wagner and his own previous experiments.

The interesting point is that, cold detached commentary as it is, a great deal of the orchestral fabric of "The Golden Cockerel" seems to have developed far more spontaneously than, for example, the fantastic pages of "Sadko" or the barbaric Tartar music of "Kitezh." There are numerous lapses; nothing could be more obviously artificial than the music of the Astrologer, the beginning of the second act, and dozens of shorter passages. But many of the ramifications of the Tsaritsa's theme sound like the natural unfolding of musical thought, controlled only to a normal extent by the composer's conscious mind. Even in some passages where the composer's quasi-mathematical intelligence is definitely in charge (as in the wedding march in the third act) the mosaic patterns are inlaid with such skilful ease that their artificiality is almost perfectly concealed. If the themes do not come to life and move of their own accord, the puppets are controlled so naturally that one almost takes them for actors of flesh and blood. For this reason, although it is lacking in the lyrical beauty of the best of the earlier operas, "The Golden Cockerel" must be given a high place in Rimsky-Korsakov's work.

Of beauty in the deeper sense of the word there is none in "The Golden Cockerel." Naturally the subject allows no scope for it. The most charming pages of the score are provided by the drowsy sleep music in Act I, particularly delightful when the drowsy melody steals back on the 'cellos, while the wood-wind delicately outline the Cockerel's motives of reassurance and warning (both transmuted here to a lulling accompaniment):—

Ex. 86

But even this brief interlude, recalled at the end of the opera when the people think regretfully of the tranquil reign of this best of rulers, will hardly bear comparison with the best pages of "Snegurochka" or "Sadko" or "Kitezh." The other definitely lyrical parts of the "Cockerel" are undistinguished, though never insipid. The spirit of folk-song impregnates the straightforward, humorous music connected with Amelfa and the fatuous princes, and actual folk-melody steps in with the welcoming chorus that follows the wedding march in Act III, one last borrowing from the treasure-hoard of popular art which the composer himself had collected.*

The songs and dances in the second act are typi-

* The melody is No. 59 of his "Hundred Russian Folk Songs."

cal of Rimsky-Korsakov's oriental music, a side of his work which, owing to the popularity of "Scheherazade" and trifles like the Hindu song in "Sadko" and the Tsaritsa's greeting to the sun in the "Cockerel," is commonly supposed to be more important than it is. Actually these, with a few songs, "Antar," and the Cleopatra episode in "Mlada" (only too clearly echoed at the beginning of the seduction scene in the "Cockerel"), represent the whole of it, a very small, though attractive, proportion of his total output. As Calvocoressi has put it, the oriental tendency of Russian composers has always been "an instinct rather than an attitude," but Rimsky-Korsakov's orientalism is rather superficial even in the two symphonic suites. He never achieved anything like the voluptuous warmth of Balakirev's "Islamey" and "Tamara," though these were evidently his models. (He approaches it most nearly in "Antar," perhaps.) Nor did he actually invent many themes of an oriental type. The melodies are either closely derived from Glinka or Balakirev (the solo violin theme of Scheherazade herself, for instance, from a melody (see Ex. 87) in "Tamara"), or are actual eastern tunes—three of the Arabian melodies in "Antar," the Persian

Ex. 87

dance in "Mlada," and others. And the composer treats these oriental and quasi-oriental themes with the same favourite harmonic formulas that he uses for the Russian folk-themes. In short, Rimsky-Korsakov's orientalism though more natural and more nearly authentic than that of any Western composer, is little more than a convention. Balakirev's and Borodin's quasi-eastern music is also conventionalised, of course, but with them the oriental influence went deeper. One has only to compare the hard, symmetrical, highly stylised arabesque patterns of the "Cockerel" with the profusion of ornament in the opening of "Tamara" or the natural efflorescence of the 'cello melody in the *andante* of Borodin's First Symphony, as it goes on, to hear the difference. What with Rimsky-Korsakov was something to be applied externally was in the cases of the other two composers a natural mental trait. But to condemn Korsakov's orientalism on that account would only be pedantic. These facts concern the critic only in so far as they help to distinguish the composers' characteristics.

After all, if Rimsky-Korsakov's orientalism gives one the impression that it is merely external, so do many of the other and more important elements of his music. They seem not to have sprung from something deep and vital in the composer, irrepressibly finding an outlet, but to have been observed by him, absorbed and coloured (but seldom wholly transmuted) by the play of an imagination at once precise and fantastic, a musical imagination literally unique in quality. The music which seems to have poured from him with natural *élan* is sometimes very beautiful and individual, but far more often weak and insipid, especially in his later works. Not infrequently the two elements are incongruously juxtaposed as in the Tsaritsa's "Hymn to the Sun," where the banality of the melody is scarcely disguised by the exotic trimmings. It may have been consciousness of the external nature of so much of his work which prompted that curious remark about art being "essentially an enchanting and intoxicating lie." It is difficult to imagine Chopin or Schubert, to say nothing of Bach or Beethoven or Mozart, coming to that conclusion even in a moment of depression. One can understand a man doubting the value of his own work in such a moment, or bitterly resenting the smallness of the reward or recognition it had brought him, but not his giving way to the thought that art itself is futile and false. Art may be only a veil of illusion drawn over the face of reality, but the illusion has very little value if it is not convincing. The great creative artists of all ages have all had this in common, that they have believed intensely in their work, in the importance and reality of art. The intensity of their belief communicates their conviction to us. Rimsky-Korsakov's fatal weakness is his self-consciousness. He sets out to create illusion, knowing all the time that it *is* only illusion. We frequently cannot believe in his music, simply because he frequently does not believe in it himself. The artist may be sceptical about anything in the world, but not about his art. Rimsky-Korsakov is a priest celebrating the rites of a religion in which he has no faith—or, at least, not the deep and burning conviction which is true faith. He enjoys doing it. He does live wholeheartedly in the ritual; it is immensely important to him. And so he makes the ceremonial itself very impressive. Quite often he works himself up to the point of temporarily convincing himself that there really is a deeper truth behind it. But the sceptic in him always triumphs over the believer. So it is, after all, more fitting that this tragedy of an over-sophisticated man should close with the question-mark of "The Golden Cockerel" rather than with the affirmation of "Kitezh."

The tragedy was a real one, for Korsakov was not always content merely to enjoy his marvellous command of the resources of music and the exercise of his inexhaustible imagination in manipulating them. He *needed* to believe. His serious breakdown of health in 1892-3 seems to have been the result of a profound inward dissatisfaction, contrasting curiously with the self-satisfaction of so many pages of his memoirs. Does not this interlude, which had echoes in later years, when the composer's "love for music cooled entirely" and he restlessly devoured systems of philosophy and æsthetics, suggest that the composer suffered from a sense of something indefinable lacking in himself, from that "melancholy of impotence" which Nietzsche imagined he saw in Brahms, very much as Snegurochka was tormented by her lack of human warmth? His case is one of the most curious in the history of music.

XV.—BALAKIREV: A FLAWED GENIUS.

BALAKIREV is one of the great enigmas of music. His shadow lies over the whole of the "classical" period of Russian music. During the dozen or so years following Glinka's death he was, next to the Rubinstein brothers, the most prominent figure in the world of Russian music, without exception the most vital. Yet all through this period, in spite of his generally acknowledged creative gifts and his position as leader and mentor of a group of composers, he actually wrote comparatively little. Then after a quarter of a century or more of almost complete silence, came another period of nine or ten quiet, but comparatively fruitful, years. Balakirev was born before Queen Victoria came to the throne of England and died only four years before the outbreak of the Great War. He had known Glinka personally, yet before he died Stravinsky had written "The Fire Bird," a ballet on the subject he had considered from an operatic point of view far back in the 'sixties. He had bullied Rimsky-Korsakov and Tchaïkovsky and Borodin and Mussorgsky, interfered in the composition of their works, helped them, exasperated them and outlived them all. Without Balakirev the Kuchkisti would all have been different and lesser men; they might even have failed to become composers at all. Even Tchaïkovsky was under a heavy debt to him. Yet his own position as a composer is strangely equivocal. He was so obviously "the strongest personality of his circle," as Tchaïkovsky told Madame von Meck, that one feels he ought to have been the greatest of all Russian musicians, instead of the brilliant failure he is generally considered.

It is easy to see why Balakirev lost the position of social leadership in the musical world which was naturally his. He seemed to be marked out by destiny as a sort of Russian Liszt; for there is an obvious similarity between the two men, even as composers. But Balakirev lacked one of Liszt's assets and one of his useful weaknesses, his unfailing charm of manner and his tendency (whether due to polite hypocrisy or genuine kindness of heart it is difficult to say) to scatter indiscriminate praise.

Where Liszt would have praised and flattered, Balakirev condemned and bullied. He was masterful and violent (if one may speak of intellectual violence), a musical Peter the Great or Ivan the Terrible, and it is easy to understand why his despotic personality repelled the sensitive Tchaïkovsky, the dry and precise Rimsky-Korsakov and even the amiable Borodin, apart altogether from his habit of criticising their compositions with brutal frankness. "Balakirev is living here," writes the twenty-nine-year-old Tchaïkovsky to his brother in 1869, "and I must confess that his society weighs on me. He is a very good fellow . . . but—I don't know why—I can never feel absolutely at home with him. I particularly dislike the narrowness of his taste and the acerbity of his tone." Rimsky-Korsakov records similar feelings; indeed many pages of his memoirs are unpleasantly flavoured with resentment against the man he had once idolised, a resentment only partly justified by his belief that Balakirev had caused him to waste years of his life in following wrong paths.

Full of a sort of demoniac enthusiasm himself, Balakirev was never happy unless he was infecting other people with his ideas, inciting them to do things and worrying them to do them differently. He seems to have put a great deal of the best of his creative self into other men and their works. He largely frittered his genius away in improvisations which he never bothered to write down, and wasted vital energy in non-creative work, concert-direction and other activities for which he was not really suited. It was only after his spiritual *volte-face*, in his retirement from active musical life and between the intervals of religious absorption, that he began to produce (and write down his earlier productions) steadily and industriously. The tragedy is that it was then almost too late.

So we find that Balakirev's compositions belong to two periods. The first consists of those of the late 'fifties and early 'sixties, works of immature genius like the Russian, Czech and Spanish Overtures, the "King Lear" music, "Russia" and the best of his songs. The period definitely closes with "Islamey" in 1868, though "Tamara," conceived long before, appeared as a dazzling afterthought early in the 'eighties. The second period opens in 1898 with the appearance of the First Symphony (begun far back in 1866), and includes another Symphony, a Piano Concerto, a Piano Sonata, and a

Cantata written for the dedication of the Glinka Memorial in St. Petersburg in 1906—works of a lonely old man living, probably, on memories of the brilliant days of forty years earlier. In Balakirev's music, therefore, we have the dawn and sunset of genius with little of its full day.

The invention of themes was not one of Balakirev's strongest points. It is curious that of all his earlier orchestral works only the "King Lear" music is based on original ideas. The others are founded on folk-songs—Russian, Spanish or Czech. All three themes of "Islamey" are borrowed from Caucasian and Armenian sources. The theme of the first *allegro* of "Tamara" is an oriental melody which he and Rimsky-Korsakov heard in the barracks of the Imperial Escort. When he does invent them, Balakirev's own themes, though very individual, are not always of the finest quality. The chief subject of the first movement of the C major Symphony, which undergoes such extraordinary adventures in the course of the movement, is as unpromising as a theme well could be. The clarinet melody of the *andante* of the same symphony is beautiful, but not to be compared with that of the slow movement of Borodin's B minor Symphony, for example. And yet it would be absurd to say that Balakirev was unfertile or uninventive. It was only, apparently, that his creative imagination needed a given starting-point. He had genuine creative fire but he was often obliged to borrow fuel to start it. But the extraordinary conflagrations he was able to produce from remarkably little fuel provide ample evidence of his inventiveness. The symphonic poem, "Russia," and the piano fantasia, "Islamey," two works which superficially appear to have nothing in common, both show in the clearest possible light the nature of Balakirev's genius. Something has already been said of "Russia" in discussing Balakirev's treatment of folk-songs. "Islamey," very much more than the mere virtuoso-piece it appears to be, shows even more clearly the special quality of Balakirev's creative power, though that power is not easy to define in words. Principally, it consists of ability to build round the thematic nucleus a wealth of sound, materially derived from it but essentially the stuff of the composer's glowing imagination. In some respects this reminds one of Rimsky-Korsakov. But Balakirev has that warmth and exuberance in reality which Rimsky-Korsakov only seems to have. Whereas

Rimsky-Korsakov's sensuousness is almost always cold and well under control, Balakirev's is warm, passionate and insufficiently restrained; comparison of "Scheherazade" with "Tamara" shows the difference most graphically. Balakirev is what Goethe used to call *dämonisch*, exuberantly following his every impulse without check. In this, the intensity with which he lives in the present moment, he reminds one of Tchaïkovsky, except that Tchaïkovsky's intensity of feeling is definitely emotional and expressive, while Balakirev's is purely musical, a keen savouring of melody, harmony, rhythm and timbre. Just as some epileptics are said to have unnatural brilliance and clarity of vision in the moments before a fit, Balakirev often seems to have "seen" his musical material with almost morbid intensity.

Having handed on to Tchaïkovsky in a letter an idea "which had just accurred to him involuntarily" for the other's "Romeo and Juliet" Overture, he continues: "If I were going to write the overture I should take fire from this germ and I should brood over it, or rather bury it in the depths of my mind—and then something vital would come of it." That is interesting and significant. But unlike the great German masters who have done wonders with unpromising material, Balakirev seems less to discover and exploit the hidden possibilities of his themes, than to see in them pretexts for unloosing the flood of his own imaginings. And his exuberance is not checked by technical limitations. His musical speech is easy and assured. The brilliance of his scoring is hardly surpassed even by Rimsky-Korsakov, and in his exploitation of the resources of piano colour he ranks not far below Chopin and Liszt and Debussy. "Islamey," with all its hideous difficulties, is splendidly pianistic. For all its lavishness, there is no squandering. Every note tells. The piece is, admittedly, a *tour de force*, but there is nothing in it that is not musically essential, no display for the sake of display.

These great natural gifts were crippled not by technical incompetence but by external circumstances and defects inherent to the composer's mental constitution. The history of the prolonged composition of "Tamara" is enlightening. According to Rimsky-Korsakov a "considerable part" of it had already been "improvised together" in 1866-7, and often played by the composer to him and other members of their circle. In October, 1869, Balakirev himself writes to Tchaïkovsky that his last letter "made me feel so jolly that I went for a walk on the Nevsky Prospect, hopped and skipped, and even composed something for my 'Tamara.'" A little later Rimsky-Korsakov reports the complete abandonment of Balakirev's creative activities (specially referring to the interruption in the composition of "Tamara") owing to pressure of other work. Then came Balakirev's first period of complete withdrawal from the musical world, the period when as Tchaïkovsky put it he "suddenly became pious, and spent all his time in church, fasting and prostrating himself before relics—and nothing else." But at the very period (1878) when Tchaïkovsky was writing in these terms to Madame von Meck, Balakirev returned to his old musical life and again took up "Tamara." Even then the work progressed very slowly and this not exceptionally long symphonic poem was not finished till 1882, fifteen years after a "considerable part" of it had been invented (though apparently not written down).

In view of this mental and spiritual restlessness of Balakirev's, this inability for one reason and another to concentrate on creative work, his reproach to Tchaïkovsky for the latter's "inactivity due to lack of concentration" seems almost humorous. But interruptions of this kind are not enough in themselves to account for the delay in the completion of "Tamara," especially when one considers how little ground there is for Rimsky-Korsakov's complaint of its fragmentariness. As a matter of fact, neither "Tamara" nor the C major Symphony bears obvious traces of its protracted birth. Part of the explanation probably lies in Balakirev's peculiar method of composition, the planning in advance of a definite whole and then the "brooding," improvising method of filling in the separate parts. His account to Tchaïkovsky, in the letter already quoted from, of his process in the composition of his "King Lear" Overture is an invaluable revelation: "Having first read the play, I was inspired with the wish to compose an overture . . . and not yet having any materials, I fired my imagination with a general outline. I planned an introduction, *Maestoso*, and then something mystical (Kent's prediction). The introduction dies away and a stormy, passionate *allegro* begins. This is Lear himself, the discrowned, but still mighty, lion. The characteristic themes of Regan and Goneril serve as episodes, and finally the second subject of the calm and

BALAKIREV

tender Cordelia. Then the middle section (storm, Lear and the Fool on the heath), with the repetition of the *allegro*: Regan and Goneril finally crush their father, and the overture dies away softly (Lear over Cordelia's corpse); Kent's prediction—now fulfilled—is heard again, and then comes the grave and quiet death. I must explain that, at first, I had no musical ideas, but these soon came and fell into place within the framework I had devised."* Possibly the process of actual creation took no longer with Balakirev than with other composers. But he would then carry the more or less complete work in his mind for years, playing it over to his friends, "burying it in the depths of his mind," and letting it slowly ripen. Balakirev's characteristically Russian inertia and a peculiar reluctance to put things in a definite form on paper, reminding one of Borodin's hesitation with "Prince Igor," also played a part. This lassitude seems to have been of a different nature from ordinary dislike of the physical drudgery of writing out a composition, such as we know was felt by Mozart and Wagner, just as the

* Ravel has confessed to a somewhat similar plan of action in writing his sonata for violin and piano, though in his case purely musical considerations—form, style, and general character of the material—took the place of Balakirev's literary outline.

gradual natural maturing of ideas lying in the composer's brain differs from Beethoven's careful filing and polishing of themes. Perhaps it is this ripening process which is responsible for the over-richness of works like "Tamara," the lack of chiaroscuro, of background shades and low lights. Every part is almost equally rich in flavour, but at the same time one feels that the composer has lived with his most brilliant inspirations so long that he has grown a little tired of them. If "Tamara" betrays its long-drawn fœtation it is not in the unevenness of quality and lack of structural cohesion alleged by Rimsky-Korsakov but in the general over-ripeness of its texture.

The case of the First Symphony in C major is even more remarkable than that of "Tamara" for, according to Rimsky-Korsakov, at least a third of the first movement was in score and sketches had been made for the scherzo and finale as early as 1866, though the finished score bears the date "April 23rd, 1898." Yet it is almost impossible to say what was written by the Balakirev of twenty-nine and what by the Balakirev of sixty-one, and the other late works give one surprisingly little help in this respect. The fiery "Scherzo alla Cosacca" and the brilliant finale of the Second Symphony (1908) have all the heroic exuberance of the compositions of nearly half a century earlier.* Balakirev, unlike Rimsky-Korsakov, had not advanced with the times; his latest music still belonged harmonically to the middle of the nineteenth century. And yet he was in no sense repeating himself. Nearly all his themes are stamped with the impress of his vivid musical personality, yet there are none of those hardly disguised resuscitations which irritate one in Rimsky-Korsakov's music. The first movement of the C major Symphony differs from the rest of his work only in its more pronounced intellectual character. It is first and foremost a piece of musical thinking. Like Borodin's E flat Symphony it begins with a slow passage which, far from being a mere introduction, is a vitally important statement of material. The apparently insignificant opening bars :—

* Some of the material, at least, of this scherzo was actually originally intended for the First Symphony.

contain the germs (a) and (b) of practically the whole of the first movement, a movement so ingeniously spun that almost a bar by bar analysis is necessary to unravel it. This may have been one of the reasons why Balakirev abandoned the symphony for so many years. He probably lost himself in an intellectual labyrinth. The problems to be solved here were not of the kind that could be cleared up by "brooding." And so when he came back to them in later years, he dealt with them rather cavalierly, riding rough-shod over difficulties. There is very little left of conventional sonata-form, but a definite design emerges from the musical argument —and the urgent sweep of the movement carries conviction. The composer plunges boldly ahead, pushing over the dry patches by force of intellect, heedless of the banality of some of the (very unimportant) subsidiary material, much as in the last movement he relentlessly drives his not very well matched themes side by side in rough counterpoint

Ex. 88a, after a bad unison beginning to the *allegro vivo*, soon surprisingly comes to life and effectively dominates the whole movement. Ex. 88b becomes by turns argumentative and heroic :—

Ex. 89

and later undergoes still more striking metamorphoses. There is nothing consciously self-expressive about the music and yet in this unswerving logic (a sort of doctrinaire logic-without-commonsense), developing what is essentially only a single idea with such pertinacity, yet with such natural exuberance, taking very little notice of side-issues but full of curious little twists and pivotings of thought (like the "enharmonic puns"), it is surely not too imaginative to see the brilliant, narrowly dogmatic, argumentative Balakirev who oppressed Tchaïkovsky and irritated Rimsky-Korsakov.

After a restless, enigmatic scherzo comes a rather luscious *andante* in D flat.* None of Balakirev's idiosyncrasies is more noticeable than this perpetual tendency to gravitate to the keys of D and D flat and their relative minors, and to contrast them as if they were closely related—a trait which, as we have seen, made an impression on Borodin. Balakirev's affection for these keys left its marks on the other members of the "Kuchka." In his own case it almost amounted to a mania, for the greater part of practically everything he wrote is in D, D flat, B minor or B flat minor.† Even in this Symphony, nominally in C major, the last tremendous clinching

---

* Judging from a remark of Yastrebtsev's, this movement was originally intended for a *Third* Symphony! It is characteristic of Balakirev that he should be planning a Third Symphony before even the First was put on paper.

† "Balakirev really likes no keys but D flat major and B minor," Rimsky-Korsakov once remarked to Yastrebtsev.

restatement of Ex. 88a, thundered out *fortissimo* in semibreves just before the end of the first movement, is in B flat minor and the final C major trumpetings hardly restore the tonal balance. And so the slow movement is in D flat (reached ingeniously through the tonic major close of the A minor scherzo) and the second subject of the finale in D; and one is consequently less surprised than one ought to be on finding that the first movement of the Second Symphony, otherwise conventional enough in design, has drifted within forty bars of the opening from D minor to D flat major. The mannerism is not only rather exasperating in itself but does a great deal to give a false impression of the want of variety in Balakirev's music.

It is this lack of balance, this inability to resist an artistic temptation, which more than anything else prevents Balakirev from taking a place in the front rank of symphonic composers. There are other weaknesses, admittedly. The *andante* of the First Symphony, beautiful as it is, has not symphonic breadth and dignity. And the corresponding movement, the *romanza*, of the Second is one of Balakirev's weakest creations, little more than an orchestral "song without words." (In fact one of its themes seems to have been devised purely with an eye to its use in the finale.) The chief theme of the polonaise of the Second :—

Ex. 90

strikes one at first as more suitable for the finale of a suite than of a symphony. But the nervous energy of the melodic rhythm grows on one. Its peculiarities are seen to be essential, not merely decorative as they appear at first. There is just enough suggestion of the second subject of the first movement to show that they belong to the same family, and by the time the folk-song theme appears on the *cor anglais* :—

Ex. 91

one accepts the symphonic nature of the movement without question.

But when all Balakirev's limitations as a symphonic composer are admitted, it is difficult to understand why these two fine works are neglected as they are. But conductors, like most prominent musical executants, are notoriously unwilling to play works which are neither established classics nor contemporary novelties, and an overlooked composer like Balakirev stands a poor chance of recognition except as the result of persistent propaganda by a devoted champion. (An isolated performance now and again is of little use.) Yet his symphonies could hardly fail to be welcomed in a world which has not yet grown tired of Tchaïkovsky's and still listens with a certain amount of pleasure even to Schumann's. The fact that they must have sounded a little old-fashioned when they appeared would not weigh with modern audiences. They are old-fashioned now only in the sense that they bear the marks of a period, as all music does. The circumstance that the period is that of the composer's youth instead of that of his old age is only accidental, the result of his curiously interrupted career.

But Balakirev, though living in the past during these concluding years of his life, was not content tamely to accept old conventions. The first movement of the C major Symphony is not the work of a radical-turned-conservative, and the B flat minor Piano Sonata shows the composer experimenting just as eagerly with new forms as he had done forty years before. Indeed the design of its *andantino* first movement is more adventurous than that of anything else he wrote. It is, in effect, a reconciliation of fugue with sonata-form—or at least with its broad outline of statement, development and recapitulation. And it is followed by a mazurka, charming but so long that it upsets the balance of the sonata as a whole,* and a curious, enigmatic *larghetto* "intermezzo," the theme of which reappears in the fiery finale. Yet for all this looseness of build the sonata is a real sonata; very free, but by no means the mere concatenation of separate pieces it superficially appears to be. Nor is there any sign of decreasing physical and inventive vigour in such themes as this one which plays an important part in the finale:—

Ex. 92.

It is true that the later compositions lack the exotic glamour of "Islamey" and "Tamara," the

* Actually the mazurka was written first, as a separate piece, and the other movements were, so to speak, composed round it.

sheer wizardry which in those works conjures up such splendid fabrics of sound from the slightest basic material. Except the scherzo of the Second Symphony they have not the epic hardness and terseness, the bold, clear-cut outline of "Russia." But in compensation they have greater breadth and more sustained power. It seems that continuous creative activity, like that of a normal composer, spread over that tragic blank of more than twenty years—blank but for the completion of "Tamara," that is—could hardly have failed to produce a series of masterpieces of the first rank.

But Balakirev was abnormal in almost every respect. He and Rimsky-Korsakov present two of the most baffling enigmas which confront the student of musical psychology, though their cases are entirely different. Whereas Rimsky-Korsakov seems to have composed with the cool precision of a mathematician, Balakirev threw out music very much as a volcano throws out lava, sometimes erupting at terrific heat, sometimes lying quiet, apparently extinct but actually storing up power for a fresh outburst. The superficial resemblances between Balakirev and Rimsky-Korsakov are entirely due to the latter's unconscious borrowings and conscious imitations, often frankly admitted in his memoirs. Borodin was almost equally indebted to Balakirev, but in his case there were real affinities with his mentor in his strong vein of lyricism (both were delightful song-composers), his "heroic" tendency and his power of large-scale construction. But there the parallel ends. The easy-going, level-headed scientist and man of the world, composing little and spasmodically as he did, achieved more than the fiery mystic who devoted, or could have devoted, his whole life to music. Balakirev remains an isolated phenomenon, the more remarkable the more one studies him—and most remarkable of all in his failure to gain the peaks that seem so easily within his reach.

XVI.—TCHAIKOVSKY REVALUED.

TO offer the English reader a valuation of Tchaïkovsky is rather like laying down the law about the value of an $a + b$ in which the a is the only quantity known to everybody, and b, considerably larger, is simply whatever the writer likes to say it is. Most composers are known by only a portion of their music, but in nearly every case we can say with some certainty that the proportion of their work unknown except to the specialists is poor stuff, not worth knowing, or at any rate (as in the case of many of the Bach church cantatas and the lesser known Mozart symphonies) shows us nothing of its creator that we cannot see better in the things we know. No one but a specialist need worry about Wagner's juvenilia. One might even go through life in complete ignorance of all Beethoven's violin sonatas, important as they are, without getting at all a false idea of Beethoven's music as a whole. But with Tchaïkovsky it is quite different. Judged by bulk, he was quite as much a stage-composer as a symphonist. (And I am not sure that we ought not to regard the "Pathétique" as a dramatic work with the stage-element omitted!) He wrote ten operas, to say nothing of ballets and incidental music, and of these the great majority of English music-lovers know nothing but one or two numbers from "Eugene Onegin" and perhaps "The Battle of Poltava" from "Mazeppa." After all, most of us know only three, or perhaps four, of his six symphonies; probably the first of his three string quartets and the first of his three piano concertos. The unfamiliar works are not merely an extension of the Tchaïkovsky we know only too well; many of them show quite another side of his musical nature. The earlier operas, particularly "Vakula the Smith," and the first two symphonies show a more intimate sympathy with folk-music than do any of the later works where the folk-tunes have the effect of flies in amber. Nor is the "Casse Noisette" Suite really typical of Tchaïkovsky's lighter, lyrical vein; it consists of too much icing and too little cake to be a fair specimen. Except Handel, during the long period when he was remembered in this country by hardly anything but his oratorios, no composer of such importance has been seen so one-sidedly as Tchaïkovsky.

I do not suggest that the Tchaïkovsky everyone knows is not the best Tchaïkovsky, though the "Pathétique" certainly seems to be the product of over-ripe genius rather than of genius in maturity. I should rather regard the Fourth Symphony as, in many respects, the peak of Tchaïkovsky's musical achievement, the two later ones as psychological (or pathological) studies. In them the composer is no longer quite his natural musical self—only the abnormal Tchaïkovsky happens to be more interesting than the normal, healthy one. To avoid quibbling about purely musical quality and the interest of musical neurosis, let us put it that it is this later Tchaïkovsky which embodies most of what makes his contribution to music so individual and which ensures its lasting interest. But to base one's conception of his output as a whole on these last over-strained compositions is to see his work in totally wrong perspective, even to give a false colour to one's judgment of such hackneyed products of Tchaïkovsky's earlier days as the B flat minor Concerto and the "Romeo and Juliet" Overture. To restore the balance, to get Tchaïkovsky in proper focus, one must always keep in the back of one's mind recollection of that vast quantity of not very distinguished but always natural and unforced lyrical music which is as definitely the essential Tchaïkovsky as the "Figaro" Overture is the essential Mozart. "But how," someone may ask, "is it possible to judge the B flat minor Concerto from a 'false' standpoint? Does one not judge it by itself, by its own qualities?" In this way, I think: that we tend to read into passages like the opening of the Concerto, which are really only a naïve revelling in sensuous sound-effects, a highly strung emotional significance which really does not belong to them at all. You will get a far more accurate idea of the B flat minor Concerto if you think of it as the work of a naïve and lyrical musician, with a strong leaning toward ballet music, rather than of the man whose vein of morbidity finally reduced his genius to an infinite capacity for feeling pain.

That element of "ballet music," of luscious melody and piquant rhythm and flavour, is at the heart of all Tchaïkovsky's work. How did it get there? Undoubtedly from early impressions. which planted in him a lifelong love of Italian opera and the tuneful music of such composers as Bizet,

Grieg and Délibes. His Mozart worship put a finer temper on his mind; but it is significant that he admired rather than loved Beethoven and that, of the *Kuchkisti*, he was more repelled by Mussorgsky's uncompromising realism than by the melodious insipidity of Cui. The creative faculty naturally produces from whatever seed is thrown into it, however its products may differ in appearance from the "parent." In Tchaïkovsky's case the most important seeds were the operas of Mozart—and Donizetti and Bellini; from them developed the fibres which form by far the greater part of the texture of Tchaïkovsky's musical thought. These fibres, which for convenience' sake I have followed S. I. Taneev in calling the "ballet music" element, are easy to trace through the symphonies; easier still in Tchaïkovsky's other works. They are particularly obvious in the scherzo and parts of the first movement of the First Symphony, in the two middle movements of the Second, throughout almost the whole of the Third. It is something more than a coincidence that the pizzicato scherzo of the Fourth was written shortly after Tchaïkovsky had made the acquaintance of the score of "Sylvia." When a little later he heard "Sylvia" for the first time on an orchestra he was moved to write that "nothing during the last few years has delighted me like 'Carmen' and this ballet of Délibes."* And it is significant that he cites "Sylvia" as an example of good music written for the ballet when he defends this Fourth Symphony against Taneev's complaint that "in every movement there are phrases which sound like ballet music." The very wording of the composer's reply shows (if it is anything more than an expression of annoyance) how completely he misunderstood the nature of the criticism. Does Taneev consider any lively dance melody as ballet music? If so, what has he to say of dozens of pages in Beethoven's symphonies? Or does he mean that parts of the symphony are "in the style of Minkus, Gerber or Pugni?" Tchaïkovsky quite failed to see *what* it was in his music that made Taneev's "inner eye involuntarily see the *prima ballerina.*" Are not the *andante* melody of the first movement of the "Pathétique" and the whole of the slow movement of the Fifth Symphony simply "ballet music" strained to an emotional expressiveness foreign to its nature?

---

* Even before this (August, 1876) he had confided to his brother his conviction that "the ballet 'Sylvia' is a thousand times finer than 'Götterdämmerung'"!

The impression of something-less-than-greatness that we get from Tchaïkovsky's biggest and most tragic works may be largely due to the fact that he had not at his command a musical speech adequate to express what he wanted to say. But it is also caused by his morbid egotism, his inability to be universal. Sharing Hardy's view of a Destiny not merely blind and indifferent, but actively hostile to man and his happiness, he had nothing of Hardy's detachment and antiseptic irony. We must allow the truth of the charge of morbidity invariably brought against Tchaïkovsky but—and it is a very important "but"—it is true of only a very small proportion of his music, though deservedly the best known portion.

The other criticisms, equally familiar, are aimed more directly at Tchaïkovsky's artistic reputation, for morbidity is no great crime and may even have a value of its own in art. He is vulgar. His ideas and his musical architecture are not genuinely "symphonic." And, in addition, he has played the part of shuttlecock in a game of battledore between critics who have warmly debated his "Russianness" —not an obviously vital point, though an interesting one. These are the reasons why Tchaïkovsky is looked at askance by the *soi-disant* intelligentsia. Let us re-consider them as objectively as possible.

What is vulgarity? Frankness of utterance, obviousness, naturalness, lack of restraint and fastidiousness? All these we must admit to be Tchaïkovskian characteristics. He is often noisy and blatant . . . But let us in fairness remember that the composer himself recognised in the Fifth Symphony, the worst case, "something repellent—patchiness, insincerity and 'manufacturedness.'" The blatancy of the last movement of the Fifth is certainly a sign of hysteria, just as certainly as the vulgarity of some of his earlier work, the opening of the B flat minor Concerto, for instance, is a token of exuberant vitality. After all, it is better to have too much life than too little. Tchaïkovsky's current of thought seems rather anæmic at times, particularly in that great "unknown quantity," but it always flows naturally, is never in any need of pumping. However banal his ideas, they seldom seem manufactured—even in the Fifth Symphony itself. The magnetic power of the "Pathétique," the unique fascination it exercises on the semi-musical, is largely due to the intensity of its life. However vulgar and sentimental some of it may be, there is not a bar in it which is not musically alive. There are few symphonies of which it can be said that they do not contain a bar of padding, a bar which was not *felt* by the composer; but the "Pathétique" is one. In this respect it is the best of all Tchaïkovsky's symphonies. He was painfully conscious of his limitations as a musical architect and confessed to Madame von Meck in 1878, "I have always suffered from my inability to round and polish the form of my works. Only after strenuous labour have I at last succeeded in making the form of my compositions correspond, more or less, with their content. In earlier days I was too careless and gave too little attention to the critical re-examination of my sketches. Consequently my *seams* always showed, and there was no organic union between the separate episodes. . . . But the *form* of my works will never be *exemplary*, for the essential qualities of my musical nature can be improved, but not completely altered"—a most just criticism of his own weakness. And ten years later he repeats the statement to the Grand Duke Constantine in almost the same words: "There is frequently *padding* in my works; to an experienced eye the stitches show in my seams, but I can't help it."

That is why Tchaïkovsky is not a really great symphonist. He lives too intensely in the parts of a work; the symphonic mind must be capable of conceiving a whole. Inability to conceive a great composition in this way is not, of course, a specifically Russian weakness; it is not even common to all Russian composers. But a tendency to think episodically instead of synoptically *is* a peculiar characteristic of Russian creative minds, of novelists, dramatists and composers alike. The present moment seems to be felt by a Russian artist with such intensity that he forgets the past and takes no heed of the future. That is why the "Pathétique," though it contains no dead matter, is not a great symphony. It does not, like Tchaïkovsky's earlier symphonies, achieve artificial shapeliness through padding and vain repetitions, but it remains a collection of episodes. (I am thinking particularly of the first movement, but the same remarks apply with even more force to the symphony considered as a whole.) They have grown together, are not patched together; yet they never form one whole, they are important only for their own sakes.

So Tchaïkovsky *is* essentially Russian in at least one respect, then? His Russianness seems so obvious to most people, yet it has been vigorously denied by some who ought to know. When Tchaïkovsky's music first burst upon Western Europe he was universally hailed as the typical Slav. Then came a reaction when people, first of all in France, then in Britain, were assured that Tchaïkovsky's music was not truly Russian in spirit, a statement which had its origin in three reasons: that it was partly true, that Cui, of the rival camp in Russia, had said so in his book, "La Musique en Russie," and that experts have a natural weakness for contradicting generally accepted opinions. We must remember that the 'sixties and 'seventies in Russia, the "period of reform" after the emancipation of the serfs, when Tchaïkovsky and his brilliant contemporaries were shaping themselves, was a period of reaction from the romantic Byronism of Pushkin and Lermontov. The Slavophile party, who believed that Russia could develop best along her own lines, not by copying Western ways of thought, were playing with the idea that the way of salvation lay in following the unconscious will of "the people," and their intellectuals, Tolstoy and poets like Nekrassov and Nikitin, were indulging in a sort of *muzhik*-worship of which Mussorgsky's "Boris" was one of the chief artistic products. Even their opponents, the progressive "Westernizers," had no patience with the old sentimental romanticism; their attitude toward it is clearly expressed by the hero of Turgenev's "Fathers and Sons." Tchaïkovsky, therefore, definitely belonging by his sympathies to this past age, cuts an isolated figure among his contemporaries. He owed his original popularity in his own country to the admiration of the numerous people of ordinary intelligence and not too fastidious taste who cared nothing for intellectual fashions; to the same class, in fact, equally innocent of artistic snobbery and artistic discernment, who still think very highly of him in England. But for that popularity he had to pay by the undeserved abuse of the progressive intellectuals, just as he had to pay for his alleged Western sympathies by the abuse of the Slavophiles. Far too much, however, has been made of these contemporary criticisms by later French and English writers. We to-day ought to be able to see that, although Tchaïkovsky was a romantic and an individualist in an age which admired realism and "the people," he was at heart, if not superficially, as Russian as the narrowest of nationalists. The question of his attitude to folk-music has already been touched on. He borrowed freely from the treasure-house of popular music, much more freely than many people are aware, but his own music never acquired the accent of folk-song. So we must admit that if he thought in Russian he did not naturally express himself in Russian. But then how could he have done? The folk-idiom could hardly have been forced into the expression of passionate feeling. As for actual folk-melodies, they could only be a mask for an individualist, and as Tchaïkovsky's utterance grew more intensely personal he cared to use the mask less and less.

Tchaïkovsky's music is the counterpart of Pushkin's reflected Byronism and of Turgenev's polished prose and rather Western sentiment and outlook. It was no mere coincidence that Pushkin's masterpiece inspired his most thoroughly "Tchaïkovskian" work, "Eugene Onegin," music which, in the composer's own words, "proceeded in the most literal sense from my inmost being." The famous "letter aria" contains the essence of all that is best in Tchaïkovsky's natural musical thought. One might open the score of "Eugene Onegin" at almost any page and find music more typical of the real Tchaïkovsky than anything in the "Pathétique." How he loves to slip into dance measures! He must have revelled in the opportunities of the ball scene. One hardly needs to be told that "Eugene Onegin" was written at the same time as the Fourth Symphony. Tchaïkovsky was then in full command of his resources; his melodic flow was never fuller or more spontaneous; and, except in the one instance of "Francesca da Rimini," he had not yet begun to strain after the sensational. But there is nothing subtle about the music of "Onegin" and the F minor Symphony; it stands on no pedestal of remoteness and distinction. That is why one tires of any particular work of Tchaïkovsky's; there is nothing beneath the surface. Some of his most characteristic melodies, the love-theme in "Romeo and Juliet" or the G flat melody that appears on the first violin in the *Andante funebre* of the Third String Quartet, are as obvious as anything in good ballet music; their value lies in their warm life, in their absolute spontaneity.

And Tchaïkovsky's orchestration has just the same qualities of obviousness and naturalness. We no longer feel that his scoring is outstandingly brilliant. But on the whole, apart from his outbursts of sheer brutal noise, it wears very well. His high lights are dimmed beside those of Rimsky-Korsakov and later men, but some of his warm, delicate effects are still unsurpassed in their rather luscious way. (I am thinking especially of many pages of "Onegin" and of "The Sleeping Beauty.") Here again, it is the "ballet" effects—the fluttering accompaniments, the simple lines of pizzicato scale drawn across a melody, the little demisemiquaver rushes of wood-wind trimmngs—which always seem to be the most characteristic of Tchaïkovsky's orchestral mannerisms.

What can one conclude from all this? A great melodic gift and a wonderful flair for orchestration; a mediocre harmonic sense; a certain ability to mesmerise by persistent rather than subtle rhythms; little power of development or genuine architecture, but a marvellous power of filling a big canvas with living music. These are not the qualifications of a first-rate symphonic composer. Together with Tchaïkovsky's almost unrivalled power of rhetoric, of telling a tale of little meaning with strong words, they seem to point to the theatre as his proper sphere. But in opera, as in the symphony, Tchaïkovsky had a fatal weakness, inability to escape from himself and his own feelings. "Onegin" succeeds *because* it is subjective. The composer could see something of himself in each of Pushkin's two chief characters, in Tatyana and in Eugene himself. Both in opera and in the big instrumental forms which he needed for the deployment of his ideas, he was hampered by conventions. He was not master enough to find a natural-seeming compromise between his ideas and the conventions (to invert Goethe's phrase, Tchaïkovsky's lack of mastery shows itself in his inability to accept limitations), and not strong enough to hammer out new conventions for himself. The obvious way out, the symphonic poem, suited Tchaïkovsky no better than the symphony; it only substituted one kind of "given" framework for another. He laid out sections of music to fit a vague literary programme in precisely the same way that he laid them down to fit into the outline of sonata-form. It was not until the "Pathétique" that he broke through to freedom, to a form which arose naturally from the development of his ideas, and even then the break through was emotional rather than artistic. We hear an excited man throwing off restraint rather than an artist conquering his difficulties. But that does not matter to those who find an artist more interesting than his art. Tchaïkovsky will always be ranked higher by them than by those who care immensely for art and very much less for artistic personalities.

INDEX.